A Link in the Great Chain

A Link in the Great Chain

A History of the Chemung Canal

Gary Emerson

Published by Purple Mountain Press
Fleischmanns, New York

for the Chemung County Historical Society
Elmira, New York

*I dedicate this book to my wife, Cindy,
and my two children, Brian and Christie, for all of their
support and understanding.*

A Link in the Great Chain: A History of the Chemung Canal
First Edition 2004

Published by
Purple Mountain Press, Ltd.
1060 Main Street, P.O. Box 309, Fleischmanns, New York 12430-0309
845-254-4062, 845-254-4476 (fax), purple@catskill.net
http://www.catskill.net/purple
and
The Chemung County Historical Society
415 East Water Street, Elmira, New York 14901-3410
607-734-4167, 607-734-1565 (fax), cchs@chemungvalleymuseum.org
http://www.chemungvalleymuseum.org

Library of Congress Control Number: 2005924793
ISBN 1-930098-48-0

4 3 2 1

Manufactured in the United States of America on acid-free paper

CONTENTS

Acknowledgements

I would like to thank the Chemung County Historical Society, the Montour Falls Memorial Library, and the Schuyler County Historical Society for their help in locating the sources for this work. I also greatly appreciate the the tremendous assistance given to me by Craig Williams at the New York State Archives.

Introduction

ON JULY 4, 1830, A HUGE CROWD filled the streets in Elmira near the courthouse. The Fourth of July had always been marked with festive celebration, but this one was different. This marked the day that the construction for the long-awaited Chemung Canal was begun. People from all around the surrounding area had come to Elmira to witness the event and celebrate the prosperity it promised to bring. While guns boomed in revelry, the celebrants consumed whiskey in large quantities.

The crowd marched in a procession from the courthouse to the ground-breaking site near the Chemung River. Standing on a platform erected for the purpose, James Robinson made a speech that recounted the battle in the legislature that had won them the right to construct the canal. Just before the speech, 13 former soldiers from the American Revolution, chosen from Elmira, Horseheads, and other surrounding communities, had ceremonially taken shovels and picks in hand to dig the first dirt on the Chemung Canal line. The great project had begun.[1]

The Chemung Canal became one of several canals built in the 1830s in New York State to capitalize on the widely successful Erie Canal, which had opened in 1825. By connecting the Chemung River to Seneca Lake at Jefferson (Watkins Glen), the Chemung Canal became a link in the great chain of canals across New York. The Chemung Canal allowed boats to access the Erie through the Cayuga and Seneca Canal located at the northern end of Seneca Lake. It was believed that easy access to eastern markets would bring plentiful and cheaper goods to Elmira and the other towns along the Chemung Canal. In exchange, the Elmira and Corning area would send large quantities of lumber and agricultural

---

1 "Ground-Breaking for Canal 'Great Day' in 1830." *Elmira Telegram*, July 4, 1885. Reprinted in *The Chemung Historical Journal*, vol. 1, no. 4, (June, 1956):166. The thirteen men symbolized the original thirteen states; *Geneva Gazette and Mercantile Advertiser*, July 21, 1830, p. 3. This paper gave an account of the groundbreaking at Elmira and included some of the toasts that were given.

products to New York, Albany, and other cities along the Erie Canal. One of the most important commodities the Chemung Canal would make available to the market was the vast quantity of Pennsylvania coal that lay just across the border near Elmira and Corning.

The Chemung Canal linked distant markets, but it also linked two eras: agrarian and industrial. The canal brought social and economic changes that had a tremendous impact on the communities along the canal. It created a society that the railroads would bring to fruition.

Before the canal could be built, legislative approval had to be obtained. Although a bill to construct the Chemung Canal had been first introduced in the state legislature in 1825, it did not gain final approval until 1829. Politics, jealousies, and competition all played a part in delaying passage. Local advocates for the Chemung Canal found allies in communities that hoped to profit from the canal. They found enemies in areas distant from the chain of canals, where people resented large expenditures on internal improvements that promised no direct benefit to their region. The Erie Canal's extraordinary success, and the desperate need for a better means to transport goods in large quantities to distant markets, convinced the people and the legislature to pass the Chemung Canal bill.

Building the canal was not without obstacles. Geography, labor problems, contractual difficulties, flooding, and improper construction contributed to delaying its completion. Although construction was anticipated to take only two years, it took over three years to complete the work. The many problems the project confronted portended future chronic difficulties that ultimately shortened the canal's life.

When the canal finally opened, it brought important economic and social impacts. The canal gave local areas access to markets that had been inaccessible. Communities along the Chemung Canal sent coal, lumber, plaster, salt, and agricultural products to Buffalo, Rochester, Albany, and New York and received manufactured goods in return. The populations in Elmira, Corning, Havana (Montour Falls), and Watkins Glen grew as business boomed. Sawmills, gristmills, groceries, pottery works, banks, boatyards, and foundries were among the businesses spawned locally by the canal. The economy, land values, and even land use changed due to the Chemung Canal.

While the groundbreaking celebrants eagerly anticipated the future economic benefits the canal would bring, they failed to anticipate the social effects. Increased contact with distant areas brought diseases to their doorstep. The need to build and maintain the canal brought an influx of workers, mainly immigrants from Ireland. The canal laborers and the workers in the newly created industries combined to create a wage-earning working class dependent on their jobs and their employers. The poverty, working conditions, and drinking habits that characterized the workers contributed to greater crime and social tensions. Middle- and upper-class citizens worried about the habits that characterized the working poor. Foul language, intemperance, crime, and failure to observe the Sabbath were among the complaints lodged against the workers as communities discovered that not all progress was positive in nature.

Canal business prospered and grew until the railroads arrived. Competition with the railroads marked the Chemung Canal's decline after 1850. The advantages of speed and year-round shipping on the railroads spelled doom for the canal, but the railroads alone did not cause the canal's decline. The decision to use timber locks, the frequent flood damages, and insufficient water all contributed to the high maintenance costs that brought the canal to a close in 1878.

Although the Chemung Canal had a short history, it nonetheless brought important changes. It populated the towns that stood along its banks and brought more ethnic diversity. It changed their local economies, and it changed the land. The canal acted as a bridge that transported the local area from one age into another, from an agrarian society into a new world filled with markets, money, wages, and diversity.

CHAPTER ONE

Day of Glory, Welcome Day

BUSINESS DEMANDS CREATED THE NEED for the Chemung Canal. The nascent market revolution that overtook the nation after 1815 demanded improved transportation. Merchants and farmers needed a better way to send goods to distant markets and to receive goods in return. Shipping by road proved expensive, and river transportation involved hazards that made it unreliable and risky. Poor transportation explains why many men who fought so hard for the Chemung Canal were merchants and businessmen. A canal meant faster shipping, more goods, and more profits.

Business created the demand for the canal, but politics made it a reality. Just as the market revolution influenced the economy, it also influenced politics. Promoting commercial growth became an important government function. The public demanded the government fulfill that role by financing and building internal improvements.[1]

Getting the canal built first meant gaining approval and funding from the New York legislature. That presented several obstacles. The Erie Canal's success made internal improvements popular in New York State. Many communities suddenly wanted a canal that would connect to the Erie. Gaining authorization for the Chemung Canal meant overcoming competing canal routes and the local jealousies guarding those routes. Another obstacle centered around whether the Chemung Canal would benefit the public. Would the canal's economic benefits justify its expense? Some legislators balked at building the canal if it meant trade would be directed south into Pennsylvania and Maryland rather than New York.

---

1 Charles Sellers, *The Market Revolution* (New York: Oxford University Press, 1991), pp. 5–6, pp. 31–33.

The drive and vision provided by men in Elmira, Bath, and Geneva made the Chemung Canal a reality. Their efforts convinced the legislature that the Chemung Canal would mainly boost the New York economy. Since the canal would also promote more business and traffic on other state canals, important allies in the legislature helped secure approval for the Chemung Canal.

The Chemung Canal's short length raised another issue. Would the canal do enough business and generate enough toll revenue to offset its expense? The legislature had to be convinced that the Chemung Canal would benefit more than just a local area and that it would be profitable. By itself, such a short canal would have been unprofitable, but linked with the other state canals, it promised an opportunity to forge a mighty commercial network. The canal system offered a solution to the transportation problem facing merchants and businessmen across the state.

Water transportation offered the best method to transport goods and produce. Roads were rough and unreliable. A traveler through central New York State in 1816 commented that the road he traveled over "was a great causeway formed of trunks of trees and so sparing had the inhabitants been of their soil, that we could by our feelings have counted every tree we jolted over."[2] Even the mail had difficulty getting through due to poor road conditions. In 1828 a Geneva newspaper reported, "The excessively bad condition of the Roads for most of the season past, occasioned by unusual openness of the weather, has greatly retarded the Mails in every direction."[3]

A wagon was no match for a boat when it came to hauling large tonnage. Transporting goods by road was expensive. From 1800 to 1819, shipping by wagon averaged thirty cents a ton per mile. By the time the Erie Canal opened in 1825, wagon rates averaged fifteen cents a ton per mile. Shipping goods across the Atlantic from Europe to the United States cost the same as shipping goods 30 miles by wagon in the United States. It made sense to ship goods only a short distance by road.[4]

River transport offered an alternative to shipping by roads; however, that too had its drawbacks. Many rivers were navigable only short times during the year and often involved great risks. Each spring, Steuben and Tioga County residents (Tioga County included Elmira before Chemung County was formed) counted on the high water in the Chemung River and its tributaries to transport products to the Susquehanna River. Large wooden craft called arks were built to transport the goods. These craft could only navigate the river when the water was high in the spring, and the fast-moving water posed great danger. One estimate claimed that five percent of the arks were lost on the Susquehanna each year as they journeyed

2 Carol Sheriff, *The Artificial River: The Erie Canal and the Paradox of Progress, 1817–1862* (New York: Hill and Wang, 1996), p. 17.
3 *Geneva Gazette and General Advertiser*, March 26, 1828, p. 3.
4 Spiro G. Patton, "Canals in American Business and Economic History: A Review of the Issues," *Canal History and Technology Proceedings* (March 28, 1987): 6.

down the river to Baltimore. A petition to the New York State legislature in 1825, seeking approval to construct the Chemung Canal, explained the problems arks confronted on the Susquehanna River:

> The navigation down the Susquehanna is inconvenient, expensive, and hazardous; and after arriving within 60 or 70 miles of tide water, the river becomes one of the most rapid, rocky and dangerous torrents upon which property was ever risked. . . . Notwithstanding every care and precaution, Arks, in descending the River, are not infrequently sunk, or dashed upon shoals and rocks, and the cargoes either partially or totally lost. . . . [T]here is in this further disadvantage, that it is navigable but a very small part of the year—generally from 3 to 4 weeks at most.[5]

River levels were too low during the remaining months for the 80-foot-long by 17-foot-wide arks burdened with 40 tons of goods. With so many men bringing their goods to market at the same time, the prices they received in return remained low. One contemporary newspaper commented about shipping by arks: "Such disadvantages are sufficient to discourage the most enterprising, and to paralize [sic] the energies of the most industrious population."[6]

A canal connecting the Chemung River to Seneca Lake would lengthen the shipping season and provide a less dangerous, more reliable means to transport goods to market. It also promised an even larger market. Relying on the Susquehanna meant shipping would only go south, but a canal that connected with the Erie Canal via Seneca Lake and the Cayuga and Seneca Canal would enable trade to travel north, west, and east as well. A large market could be opened with goods flowing in many directions.

A canal would make more goods available by ending the isolation that stymied trade. Many residents from the western districts in New York State depended on trade with peddlers to get needed supplies for each season. Customers often complained that peddlers cheated them. One merchant grumbled, "Pedlars have, for a long period of time, been in the habit of realizing immense profits by impositions on the community."[7] Constructing the Chemung Canal would make available to the people in Newtown (Elmira), Horseheads, Corning, Havana (Montour Falls), and Jefferson (Watkins Glen), as well as those in nearby communities, greater supplies from various sources, including New York City, Philadelphia, and Baltimore. Access to cities on the seaboard would also allow them to receive goods from overseas. A whole new world beckoned if the Chemung Canal could be built.

5 *Geneva Gazette*, February 2, 1825, p.2.
6 *Geneva Gazette and General Advertiser*, September 12, 1827, p. 3.
7 *Geneva Palladium*, January 19, 1825, p. 2.

The notion to create artificial waterways and extend inland navigation in New York State, including the Chemung Canal, began germinating during the American Revolution. General John Sullivan, along with General Clinton, led an expedition to destroy Iroquois villages in central and western New York State during the Revolution. Sullivan wrote a letter to George Washington in 1779, speculating about linking the Great Lakes to the rivers in New York and Pennsylvania by a network of canals. One route suggested by General Sullivan would later become the Chemung Canal.[8] Washington needed little convincing, as he had long advocated canals. In 1784, Washington wrote that the people living in the western regions "would embrace with avidity our Markets, if we should remove the obstructions which are at present in the way to them . . . extend the inland Navigation as far as it can be done with convenience—and shew [sic] them by this means, how easy it is to bring the produce of their Lands to our Markets, and see how astonishingly our exports will be increased."[9]

As president, Washington suggested that Congress should investigate implementing General Sullivan's suggestion, but nothing was done. In 1807, Albert Gallatin, the secretary of the treasury, relied on Washington's and Sullivan's proposal in an attempt to generate interest in connecting the waterways but found no support from the national government for such a project.[10] It was becoming clear that if any canal was to be built, New York State would have to take matters into its own hands.

The New York State legislature created a Board of Canal Commissioners and authorized it to explore possible canal routes. In 1812, James Geddes, an engineer and judge, explored a potential route between Seneca Lake and the Chemung River (then known as the Tioga River). Geddes confirmed the route's practicality, and, consequently, the state had the route surveyed.[11]

When still no action seemed imminent, some private citizens planned to form a company to build a canal from Seneca Lake to the Chemung River. Communities from Elmira (then known as Newtown) to Geneva at the north end of Seneca Lake supported the plan. Since the Chemung River flowed into the Susquehanna River, it was hoped that the water route linking Seneca Lake to the Chemung would open a profitable market in Pennsylvania for New York salt and gypsum.[12]

In 1815 the Seneca and Susquehannah [sic] Lock Navigation Company was incorporated. The New York State legislature limited the stock subscription to 6,000 shares at fifty dollars per share. The Pennsylvania legislature even consid-

---

8 Noble Whitford, *History of the Canal System of the State of New York, Together with Brief Histories of the Canals of the United States and Canada* (Albany: Brandow Printing Company, 1906), p. 607; "The Chemung Canal," *Geneva Gazette*, April 29, 1829, p. 3; "Chemung Canal Report," *Geneva Gazette and General Advertiser*, Feb. 18, 1829, p. 2.

9 John C. Fitzpatrick, ed., *The Diaries of George Washington*, vol. 2, (New York: Houghton Mifflin Co., 1935), p. 325.

10 "Chemung Canal Report,"*Geneva Gazette and General Advertiser*, Feb. 18, 1829, p. 2; "The Chemung Canal," *Geneva Gazette*, April 29, 1829, p. 3.

11 Whitford, *History of the Canal System*, pp. 607–8; "The Chemung Canal," *Geneva Gazette*, April 29, 1829, p. 3.

12 Ibid.

ered buying 2,000 shares in the hopes of cashing in on the increased trade the Chemung Canal would make possible. The company had 14 years to make the canal a reality or lose its right to build it; however, time ran out before it could carry out the task, and construction never began.[13] Chemung Canal proponents had been frustrated once again. Both the national government and private enterprise proved unwilling or unable to make better inland transportation a reality.

The tremendous success enjoyed by the Erie Canal would change the Chemung Canal's fortune. Construction began on the Erie Canal in 1817, and even before its completion "canal fever" had spread across New York State. Many communities wanted access to the Erie, and petitions for other canals came pouring into the state legislature. Chemung Canal advocates began to champion their cause with the New York State Assembly, hoping to gain state funding for their route. The 1824 *Assembly Journal* reported on a petition requesting a bill to authorize a canal from Seneca Lake to the Chemung River:

> Its completion would extend our salt market to the supply of the vast extent of country bordering on the shores of the Susquehanna, and the tributary navigable streams to that river, and of a considerable portion of the State of Maryland, to the amount annually of 450,000 bushels; whereas the expense of transportation now, prevents the successful introduction of our salt trade, to any considerable extent in those states . . . .[C]oal from the extensive mines in the vicinity of the navigable waters of the Tioga river, will, by means of this facility of transportation, furnish a cheap fuel for our manufactories and cities. . . .[14]

Unfortunately, the petition stimulated no action. Although construction on the Champlain Canal had already begun, the legislature would not commit to spending more on other canals until the Erie was finished and began to prove its worth. They did not have to wait long. In 1825 the newly completed Erie Canal collected over half a million dollars in tolls. The next season toll revenue reached over $750,000.[15] The Erie's incredible success proved that creating an artificial river had been a wise investment. Suddenly it seemed that every community wanted its own canal to capitalize on the wealth and prosperity a link to the Erie promised. In 1825, the New York State legislature approved surveys for 17 more potential canal routes. The Chemung Canal found itself included among the selected routes.[16]

---

13 Ibid.
14 Whitford, *History of the Canal System*, pp. 609–10.
15 George Rogers Taylor, *The Transportation Revolution, 1815–1860* (New York: Harper and Row Publishers, 1951), p. 34.
16 Carter Goodrich, *Government Promotion of American Canals and Railroads* (New York: Columbia University Press, 1960), p. 55; *Assembly Documents*, Chapter 236, April 20, 1825, New York State Library.

Getting the canal built would be a tremendous challenge. Many communities wanted a canal, but competition between routes made this difficult without political clout. If the Chemung Canal was to be built, a bill approving its creation and funding would have to pass the state assembly and senate. Representatives from areas with competing routes would try to squash its construction, fearing it would delay or kill prospects for a canal in their home districts. Jealousy, finance, and indecision would frustrate attempts to get the Chemung Canal bill passed.

From 1824 to 1828, attempts were made to gain legislative authorization to construct the Chemung Canal. Those efforts ended in failure each year. The communities hoping to benefit from the Chemung Canal needed to convince the legislature that the canal could benefit the entire state and not just their local area. Meetings were held and petitions sent off to the legislature each year, attempting to explain how the canal would impact the state economy and not just a local area. Newspapers from Elmira, Geneva, and Albany played a role in lobbying for the canal.

The battle for the Chemung Canal began at the local level. On December 28, 1824, a meeting was held at the courthouse in Newtown (Elmira). Present at the meeting were representatives from Catharine, Catlin, Veteran, Elmira, Big Flats, Southport, Erin, and Chemung Townships. They authorized a committee to write a petition to the legislature requesting a bill to construct the Seneca and Tioga Canal (the Chemung River was first known as the Tioga River). They also organized efforts to contact other communities to solicit signatures on the petition and appointed the chairman, James Sloan, to attend the upcoming legislative session to endorse the canal. Among the representatives from Newtown were William Maxwell, Isaac Baldwin, and John Arnot, who would be among the most ardent supporters of the Chemung Canal.[17]

Citizens from Steuben County met on January 8, 1825, at the Samuel Besley residence in Bath where the Tioga County petition was read and signed. They also resolved to have the newspapers in Tioga and Steuben Counties, as well as those in Albany, publish the minutes from their meeting. Dugald Cameron, who attended the meeting, would become Steuben County's leading advocate for the Chemung Canal.

Geneva, located at the northern end of Seneca Lake, had a great interest in the Chemung Canal and would become an important ally. In 1825 the legislature approved building the 20-mile-long Cayuga and Seneca Canal, giving Geneva direct access to the Erie Canal. The Chemung Canal would bring a substantial increase in traffic on the Cayuga and Seneca Canal. Canal boats locking through the Chemung Canal could be towed up Seneca Lake by steamboat to Geneva.[18] The *Geneva Gazette* published the minutes from the meetings held in Elmira and Painted Post, as well as excerpts from the *Albany Argus*, which urged support

17 *Geneva Gazette*, January 13, 1825, p. 1.
18 Ibid., April 27, 1825, p. 2.

for the Chemung Canal. Since the Chemung Canal would boost the fortunes for other canals proposed across New York State, alliances were secured which eventually pushed the Chemung Canal through the legislature.

Genevans had also called their own convention to support the Chemung Canal and urged county residents to sign the circulating petition. The final document bore signatures from citizens in Tioga, Steuben, Yates, Ontario, Wayne, Cayuga, Seneca, and Tompkins Counties. The petition reached Albany in time to plead the case for the Chemung Canal to the newly convened legislature.[19]

Many local men who led the fight for the Chemung Canal shared one thing in common. They were merchants or related to merchants. In Elmira, William Dunn, Lyman Covell, Stephen Tuttle, Isaac Baldwin, and John Arnot came from families with connections to the merchant trade. In Steuben County, Dugald Cameron's brother was the first to open a store in Bath.[20] The Maxwells and Tuttles operated mills in Elmira. Businessmen numbered among the most important canal sponsors in the hope that it would promote their businesses and increase their profits.

The 1825 petition repeated many arguments cited in the 1824 petition to the legislature. Once again the petition pointed out that the Chemung Canal would allow salt and plaster manufacturers in central New York to market their products in Pennsylvania. The petition again cited the bountiful coal fields in Pennsylvania as an important impetus for building the canal, and it added that Pennsylvania had large iron ore beds. Vincent Conklin, a Horseheads resident, went so far as to drive a wagon to the coal fields at Blossburg, Pennsylvania, load it up with coal, and haul it to Albany. There he burned the coal for witnesses to demonstrate the value the Chemung Canal would have for the entire state.[21]

The petition also argued that the canal would lower shipping costs and provide a safer means for transporting goods rather than shipping by arks. It would also make available to New York and Pennsylvania the plentiful resources the fields and forests along the proposed canal route had to offer. The petition concluded by saying:

> The proposed Canal . . .would confer superlative benefits; it would at once open a grand Highway for the safe, cheap and convenient transportation of all our marketable commodities to and from the great Emporium of our own State. The effect this would have in animating industry, in developing the resources of the country, in inviting additional popula-

19 Ibid., January 26, 1825, p. 2; Ibid., February 2, 1825, p. 2.
20 Ausburn Towner, *The History of the Valley and County of Chemung* (Syracuse, New York.: D. Mason and Company, 1892) pp. 77–78, pp. 113–115; W.W. Clayton, *History of Steuben County, New York* (Philadelphia: Lewis, Peck and Company, 1879), pp. 160–61.
21 "Letters of Uncle Jonas Lawrence," Folder 0635, Chemung County Historical Society.

tion, and in accelerating improvements of every kind, must
be powerful, and great beyond any calculation.[22]

The petition reached the assembly at approximately the same time that
another competing canal route petition reached Albany. Residents from Tompkins,
Tioga, Cayuga, and Seneca Counties hoped to connect the Susquehanna River at
Owego to Cayuga Lake at Ithaca and requested a survey for their route.[23] With so
many different requests for canal routes being made to the assembly, little action
was taken in 1825. In April 1825 the legislature gave their approval to construct the
Cayuga and Seneca Canal, thus linking Geneva to the Erie Canal, but the legislature still did not act upon the Chemung Canal. Instead, the assembly decided to
survey 17 potential canal routes to see which would be the most feasible.[24]

James Geddes once again surveyed the Chemung Canal route. Geddes
reported to the Canal Commission in 1826 that the Chemung Canal would be
easy to build and without great expense. Geddes estimated that the canal could be
completely constructed with wooden locks for approximately $240,000, or with
stone locks at $407,598. By constructing a feeder canal from Chimney Narrows
on the Chemung River (near Gibson) to intersect with the main canal at its summit level in Horseheads, an abundant water supply to operate the canal could
be made available. Geddes assured the state that the Chemung Canal would be
profitable, especially considering the products available in the forests, mines, and
fields in its vicinity.[25]

Another survey route hoped to provide a waterway from Chenango Point
to Norwich and then to the Erie Canal (later to become the Chenango Canal).
A third proposal suggested a canal connecting Owego on the Susquehanna to
Cayuga Lake. Two routes hoped to utilize the Black River to connect to the Erie
and travel northward, reaching Ogdensburg. Yet another route, later to become
the Genesee Canal, sought to link the Allegany River at Olean to Rochester and
the Erie Canal.[26] It seemed every community wanted a canal.

The survey by Geddes confirmed that the Chemung Canal would be the
most logical and economical choice among the many routes being proposed. Only
18 miles separated Seneca Lake from Elmira and the Chemung River. The topography appeared ideal. The expense would be minimal, and the rewards plentiful.
Hopes were raised among Chemung Canal supporters that the next session in the
legislature would bring victory.

For success to be achieved, Chemung Canal advocates knew they must rely
on support from legislators outside their own district to gain the majority needed
to secure passage. The assembly and the senate would have to be convinced that

22 Ibid., February 2, 1825, p. 2.
23 Ibid., February 23, 1825, p. 2.
24 Ibid., April 27, 1825; *Assembly Documents*, Chapter 236, April 20, 1825, New York State Library.
25 Whitford, *History of the Canal Systems*, pp. 610–11.
26 *Assembly Documents*, Chapter 236, April 20, 1825, New York State Library.

the canal would benefit the state at large rather than just a narrow regional interest. The bill would need allies in the legislature to convince both houses that the bill served a vital interest. Since the Chemung Canal would benefit Geneva and the Cayuga and Seneca Canal, as well as the Erie Canal, by increasing the traffic and the flow of goods, advocates hoped they could count on the votes of the representatives from those areas. The petitions that were circulated and sent to Albany from the communities along the Chemung Canal route reflected that thinking. It remained to convince the legislature that constructing the Chemung Canal would benefit the entire state.

The petitions sent to the legislature in the years after 1825 stressed how the Chemung Canal would change the direction in which trade flowed. Rather than sending produce from the region near the Pennsylvania border down the Susquehanna River, the Chemung Canal would allow that produce to travel north to the Erie Canal and then to Albany and New York City. Wheat, coal, and lumber would flow to New York State destinations, and the tolls on the Erie Canal would grow.

In 1826 the *Geneva Gazette and General Advertiser* announced that the Chemung Canal bill had passed the assembly. The newspaper celebrated the victory in the lower house and reminded its readers why they should support the canal. The Chemung Canal would spell greater benefits from the "diversion to our own markets of the production of a large and fertile section of this state and of Pennsylvania, which now seeks a market elsewhere."[27]

However, the direction goods would flow due to the Chemung Canal had become a concern. The *Buffalo Journal* criticized the proposed Chemung Canal, fearing it would drain New York produce from the state. It said: "We are at a loss to discover the advantage it would be to the state to cut a canal from the Seneca lake to the Susquehanna unless to further a vent for our productions: It could send us back no returns."[28]

Competition with other routes also hurt the chances for getting the Chemung Canal bill passed. A letter to the *Albany Argus* questioned the survey done by James Geddes. It warned that the canal would not provide good access to the Susquehanna River since the river beyond Elmira to the Susquehanna was frequently too shallow to even accommodate canoes. The letter had an ulterior motive, because it promoted a link to the Susquehanna by building a canal from Cayuga Lake to Owego rather than from Elmira.[29]

Despite the opposition, the assembly committee on canals and internal improvements reported favorably on the Chemung Canal project, and after some debate the bill passed in the assembly. Unfortunately, the assembly acted upon

27 *Geneva Gazette and General Advertiser*, December 27, 1826, p. 2.
28 Ibid., May 17, 1826, excerpt from the *Buffalo Journal*, p. 3.
29 Ibid., April 26, 1826, excerpt from the *Albany Argus*, p. 3.

it so late in the session that the senate never had time to consider the bill before adjourning for the year.[30] The bill would have to wait another year.

At a meeting at the Hemingway Hotel in Geneva on December 21, 1826, Genevans Andrew McNab, Joseph Fellows, and James Rees began preparations for the new legislature that would convene in just a few weeks. Petitions were circulated and representatives chosen to attend the legislative sessions. In Elmira, Grant and Isaac Baldwin, William Maxwell, and others attended a meeting in December 1826, and again in August 1827, to do the same. At Conkling's Hotel in Horseheads on December 12, 1826, a meeting chaired by Matthew Carpenter made resolutions to promote the Chemung Canal. Painted Post also hosted a meeting in October 1827 with Dugald Cameron serving as chairman.[31]

Realizing that the legislature lacked a local spokesman for the Chemung Canal, William Maxwell from Elmira and Jacob Swartwood from Spencer received nominations to run for the legislature. In 1826, no one from the immediate area along the canal route sat in the state legislature. The closest had been Charles Pumpelly from Owego in the assembly and John G. Spencer from Canandaigua.[32] Both Maxwell and Swartwood succeeded in their campaigns and took their seats in the assembly for the upcoming session.

In Albany, the debate in the assembly and senate revealed more objections to the Chemung Canal that would have to be countered. Assemblyman Hiram Bennett from Sullivan County spoke against the bill because, he argued, it would cost nearly $14,000 per mile to build, if made with stone locks. He doubted the projected revenue to be realized from the canal, and he thought it unwise to spend so much to construct it. Bennett also believed that it was improper for the assembly to approve the Chemung Canal when so many other routes had not been carefully considered. Only when all the other routes had been surveyed and evaluated did Bennet think the assembly should make a judgment.[33]

Assemblyman David Bucklin from Jefferson County also rose to object to the Chemung Canal. Bucklin feared the canal would draw trade from New York State by sending traffic down the Susquehanna to Philadelphia and Baltimore. Francis Granger, chairman for the committee on canals and internal improvements and friend to the Chemung Canal, defended the project. Granger reminded the assemblymen that only two days previously Bucklin had spoken against the Chemung Canal because the Susquehanna would never provide a navigable connection to the canal. Now Bucklin was contradicting himself by saying it was quite navigable and would drain the wealth from New York State.

A powerful and respected figure in the assembly, who would later be a candidate for governor in 1830 and 1832, Granger proved to be a powerful ally for

30 Ibid., December 27, 1826, p. 2; February 18, 1829, p. 2.
31 *The Geneva Palladium*, December 27, 1826, p. 2; September 12, 1827, p. 2; *Geneva Gazette and General Advertiser*, October 10, 1827, p. 2; December 27, 1826, p. 3; January 3, 1827, p. 2.
32 *Geneva Gazette and General Advertiser*, October 10, 1827, p. 3; Towner, *A History of the Valley and County of Chemung*, p. 124.
33 *Geneva Gazette and General Advertiser*, February 21, 1827, p. 3.

the Chemung Canal. Granger, from Canandaigua in Ontario County, supported the Cayuga and Seneca Canal, which would run through his home district.[34] Both Bucklin and Bennett came from districts that were remote from the Chemung Canal, and they were not about to approve a large expenditure on a canal that would have no direct benefit for their counties. Granger's position on the canal committee, and his prestige in the assembly, helped to muster votes for the Chemung Canal.

> Granger's committee reported very favorably on the proposed canal. The report said . . . the revenue to be derived from the work itself, and from the increased amount of tolls which would be collected upon the Erie canal resulting from this work would be much more than sufficient to pay the interest upon the sum required for its construction. . . . The estimate of tolls to be derived from grain, lumber, pork, beef, whiskey, pot & pearl ashes, with various other articles of productive industry going east; and from salt, gypsum, and merchandise going south amounts to about 9,000 dollars. . . .[35]

Also, when figuring in the tolls for the many boatloads of coal expected to be shipped, the Chemung Canal would yield $42,000 in tolls. Granger's committee estimated that by deducting the expenses from the revenue generated, the canal would deposit $15,000 into the New York State treasury each year.[36]

The Chemung Canal bill proved to be popular in the assembly and passed by a large margin. Sixty-seven members voted for it, and 31 sided against the bill.[37] It only needed to clear the senate to become a reality. The senate would be a more difficult hurdle.

Silas Wright, a future canal commissioner, chaired the senate canal committee. Unlike Granger's canal committee in the assembly, the senate committee provided little support or leadership to support the Chemung Canal bill. Wright gave a report to the committee that projected the costs and revenues for the Chemung Canal, but he did not express an opinion on the canal's expediency. Some objections to the Chemung Canal bill arose within the committee. Senators Latham Burrows and Samuel Wilkeson spoke against the bill. They believed the canal would harm the state by diverting traffic away from the Erie Canal. They feared that given the choice to use a canal that charged tolls, or the Susquehanna River, which had no tolls, the boaters would choose the latter. The river would siphon off traffic to Baltimore, and the Erie Canal would lose toll revenue.

---

34 *Biographical Directory of the United States Congress, 1774–Present,* http://bioguide.congress. gov. Accessed March 2000.
35 *Geneva Gazette and General Advertiser,* January 31, 1827, p. 2.
36 Ibid., February 28, p. 3.
37 Ibid., February 28, p. 3.

Senator Truman Hart defended the Chemung Canal. Hart served as a staunch advocate for the canal in the senate, and he helped to oversee its eventual passage in 1829. He pointed out that the scenario which Senators Burrows and Wilkeson worried about would not occur. Since navigation up the Susquehanna was impossible, it was unlikely that most shipments would be sent to Baltimore. Hart also reminded the committee that Wilkeson, who had referred to the Chemung Canal as a wild project, had supported even wilder schemes himself. Wilkeson had championed a canal that would connect the Erie Canal to the Allegany River. It would pass through a territory that Hart said was "so sterile that a bird of passage would be starved in an attempt to pass over it to a more hospitable region."[38]

The *Albany Argus* lent a helping hand to the Chemung Canal bill by publishing a lengthy commentary supporting its construction. Albany stood to gain from the increased business that other canals feeding into the Erie would bring. Quoting from the March 1826 report of the assembly's committee on canals and internal improvements, the *Argus* attempted to show the benefits of the Chemung Canal. The report estimated that shipments, including wheat, beef, pork, whiskey, lumber, butter, cheese, and other products, would be brought to the Hudson River, increasing tolls on the Erie by more than $25,000 annually. Estimated annual tolls on goods going south to Pennsylvania were only $3,678. Thus, the newspaper argued, the fears that the Chemung Canal would divert trade away from New York State were unfounded.

The *Argus* also trumpeted the important access to the Pennsylvania coal fields that the Chemung Canal would provide. The article stated: "The Tioga coal will . . . supply a great extent of the country with that valuable fuel, at a cheap rate." The *New York National Advocate* agreed with the *Argus* when it wrote in January 1827, "As the price of fuel is every year advancing, it must be of great importance to be insured a cheap and inexhaustible supply."[39]

The arguments advanced by Senator Hart and the *Albany Argus* could not carry the issue. The senate canal committee voted against the Chemung Canal bill with only six voting in favor of the canal. When the committee report reached the senate floor for discussion on March 21, 1827, the senate voted to sustain the committee's assessment with a 15 to 7 vote. The major objection had been a concern that the canal would not pay for itself. Unwilling to spend more than the state would get in return, the senate wanted greater assurance that the Chemung Canal would be profitable.[40]

The frustrated local people, who once again saw the senate destroy their hopes, remained convinced that government had a duty to promote the public welfare, even if it was costly to do so. A resolution passed at a meeting in Geneva

---

38 "Legislature of New-York," *Geneva Gazette and General Advertiser*, March 21, 1827, p. 3.
39 *Geneva Gazette and General Advertiser*, February 21, 1827, excerpt from the *Albany Argus*, p. 3; Ibid., January 17, 1827, excerpt from the *N.Y. National Advocate*, p. 3.
40 Ibid., March 21, 1827, p. 3; March 28, 1827, p. 3.

on January 26, 1828, stated: "Resolved, that the expenditure of a nation's funds or the use of its credit for the advancement of public prosperity, cannot be deemed a misapplication of the powers of government; and that the benefits to be derived from judicious improvements, should be sought for in the increased comfort and affluence of the people, rather than in the number of dollars and cents in their public treasury." The same document also declared that public education and internal improvements are two important functions performed by government. Education serves to "render the people sufficiently intelligent and virtuous for self government," and the internal improvements "secure their happiness and increase their enjoyments by improving their common patrimony."[41]

Determined to convince the legislature to serve the public welfare, entrepreneurs' petitions and reports to Albany for the next legislative session attempted to prove that the canal would serve the public interest. Genevan Andrew McNab and William DeZeng compiled a report to demonstrate that the Chemung Canal would serve a broad public throughout the state. Their report also addressed concerns that operating the canal would be costly due to the need to hire many lock tenders to oversee the many locks that would be required. McNab and DeZeng argued that, since the locks were so close to one another, a few men could follow the boats along the line and operate several locks, thus saving some expense. Lock tending expenses could also be defrayed by selling excess water from the canal to nearby mills for their water power.[42]

McNab and DeZeng were not satisfied merely discussing lock tenders and water power. They were more interested in the real issue: would the canal justify the large public expense required to build it? The two Genevans attempted to prove that building the Chemung Canal would be a wise decision. Their report outlined the economic bonanza the canal would make possible. The canal's revenue would not only be derived from the tolls collected, but from the tremendous traffic in trade it would generate as well. The canal would send wheat, beef, pork, whiskey, butter, cheese, and lard to markets all along the state canal system. Their report also noted the important connection to the Pennsylvania coal and iron ore fields that the Chemung Canal would make possible. McNab and DeZeng suggested that an area encompassing over 5,000 square miles and 100,000 people stood to benefit directly from the Chemung Canal.[43]

It seemed clear to the Chemung Canal's supporters that the profits it would generate justified its construction. Hopefully, it would be just as clear to the legislature. When the assembly convened in 1828, the Chemung Canal once again received a favorable report from the standing committee on canals and internal improvements chaired by Francis Granger. In presenting the report, Granger addressed the major objections that had been raised about the Chemung Canal.

---

41 Ibid., January 30, 1828, p. 3; *Geneva Palladium*, January 30, 1828, p. 2.
42 *Geneva Gazette* and *General Advertiser*, October 10, 1827, p. 2.
43 Ibid., April 2, 1828, p. 2.

One objection concerned doubts that the canal could produce enough revenue to pay for the debt the state would incur to construct and maintain it. Granger wrote, "The question then presents itself, whether this work, if constructed, would, by means of the tolls to be collected upon its own waters, and by the increase which would be created upon the Erie canal, from property thrown upon it by this channel, yield to your treasury a return equal to the expenses for its attendance and repairs, and sufficient to meet the interest upon the debt, thus to be incurred by the state." To prove his point, Granger included figures presented at previous sessions in the legislature, which gave estimates about the amount and types of products to be shipped on the Chemung Canal.[44] Coal, pig iron, lumber, salt, wheat, beef, plaster, and many other commodities all were waiting to be brought to market. How could anyone not see the wealth to be produced by the Chemung Canal?

Granger continued by addressing arguments by some detractors who insisted that the Chemung Canal would drain the produce from western New York down the Susquehanna to Pennsylvania and Maryland. He reminded them that the distance from the Chemung Canal to Albany would be less than 250 miles, while the distance down the Susquehanna to Baltimore would involve over 370 miles of canal and river travel, with an additional 70 miles by wagon to reach Baltimore. Albany would be closer and just as good a market as Baltimore, and New York City could be reached easily by navigating the Hudson River. It appeared logical that most Chemung Canal traffic would be bound for New York ports.

Another contention involved the private company formed in 1815 to construct the Chemung Canal. The Seneca and Susquehannah Lock and Navigation Company had been incorporated and sold $300,000 in stock, yet it never turned a spade of dirt. Some legislators speculated that because this private company made no effort to build the canal, perhaps the obstacles incurred made the project impracticable. If a private enterprise found the project unprofitable, then what made people think it would be any more profitable as a public project?

Granger's report noted that the economic yield would differ between a private and public enterprise. A privately operated canal would only earn the tolls it collected over the short canal route; however, the state would profit from the tolls it could collect on the Chemung Canal, the Cayuga and Seneca Canal, the Erie Canal, and any other state canal the boats should travel upon. Granger's report said, "the advantages to be derived from this work as a state project are ten-fold greater than those which it would promise to individual enterprise."[45]

The facts and figures about the canal's potential annual yields that Granger relied upon came from information supplied by Dugald Cameron from Bath. Cameron had been elected to represent Steuben County in the assembly for the 1828 session and sat listening among the delegates as Granger made his report.

44 Ibid., March 19, 1828, p. 3.
45 Ibid., March 19, 1828, p. 3.

Unfortunately, Cameron did not live to see the effects of his work. Seized by an illness while in Albany, he died before the assembly adjourned in May.[46]

Even though the committee supported the Chemung Canal bill, a battle still loomed in the assembly. The debate dragged on, causing some supporters to lose hope. The *Geneva Gazette* wrote on April 2: "[This] project . . . still lingers in the House of Assembly. It was made the order of the day for last Monday; but we fear its numerous friends will again be disappointed in their wishes."[47]

On the assembly floor, William Woods from Steuben County, Benjamin Butler from Albany, and Francis Granger defended the bill. Abijah Mann Jr. from Herkimer County, Morris Sheppard representing Yates County, Amasa Dana from Ithaca in Tompkins County, and Aaron Burt from Onondaga County led the opposition. The Chemung Canal won out in the end with a 45 to 39 vote in favor of building the canal, and the bill appropriated $300,000 to construct it.[48]

Dana and Sheppard opposed the Chemung Canal because they feared its approval would defeat plans for canals to benefit their own constituents. Sheppard supported the proposed Crooked Lake Canal from Penn Yan to Seneca Lake, while Dana championed either a canal or a railroad from Ithaca to Owego. Mann and Burt simply saw no benefit for their districts from the proposed Chemung Canal.

For a third time the bill had managed to pass the lower house, but by a much smaller margin than in earlier sessions. Once again the bill faced the senate to have its fate decided. On April 8 the senate convened to consider the Chemung Canal bill as the special order of the day. Senator Hart, still a member on the senate canal committee, defended the Chemung Canal bill. He was joined by Senators Thomas Waterman, Samuel Wilkeson, who had opposed the canal in the previous session, and Charles Carroll.

Senator William Oliver from Penn Yan in Yates County also supported the bill. He moved to amend the bill to include a passage that said: "The canal commissioners shall not enter upon the construction of said canal and feeder, until they are fully satisfied, after full examination, that the whole expense of said canal and feeder will not, when completed, exceed the sum of three hundred thousand dollars."[49] This amendment was voted down, and then the senate voted on the bill. It lost by a 15 to 11 count.

Oliver voted for the bill. So did Hart and Waterman. Those senators who voted against the bill included John Spencer from Canandaigua, George Throop, Walker Todd, and Wilkeson. Wilkeson had flip-flopped once again. He had spoken for the bill, but then voted against it. Apparently, he favored the restriction of placing a spending cap on construction costs that Oliver had tried to add.[50] Although

46 Clayton, *History of Steuben County*, p. 161.
47 *Geneva Gazette and General Advertiser*, April 2, 1828, p. 3.
48 Ibid., April 2, 1828, p. 3; April 16, 1828, p. 3; *Albany Argus*, April 12, 1828, p. 2.
49 *Albany Argus*, April 21, 1828, p. 2.
50 Ibid., April 21, 1828, p. 2.

disappointed, the *Geneva Gazette* warned: "Let the friends of this measure, which we repeat is first on the list of internal improvements, persevere—look well to the next election—and ultimate success will crown their efforts."[51]

Following the defeat in the senate in 1828, the legislature authorized another Chemung Canal survey. Since some legislators had questioned the earlier surveys done by James Geddes, a more professional survey was requested to put to rest any doubts about the canal's cost and feasibility. This time Army engineers performed the survey. Lieutenant W. H. Swift led the survey and estimated the expense to build the Chemung Canal. A Geneva newspaper commented: "Some have pretended that the former surveys were not sufficiently full and satisfactory . . . while another class resisted it with disgraceful rancor and falsehood, for no better reason . . . than it would interfere with their *local* and *private* interests. We feel persuaded that the survey now about to be by an honorable and accomplished officer, will satisfy the doubtful and silence the envious."[52]

The local men who had fought so hard for the Chemung Canal refused to give up. Once again the process began. Meetings convened in Geneva and Elmira to draft petitions and memorials to the legislature for the upcoming session. Jefferson (now known as Watkins Glen), located at the head of Seneca Lake where the canal would enter, hosted a meeting with representatives from Hector, Catlin, Tyrone, and Reading Townships in attendance. Those present at the meeting pledged their support of the efforts being made in Geneva and Elmira to make the canal a reality.[53]

The state elections in 1828 had played a role in furthering the Chemung Canal. Martin Van Buren, a canal advocate, won election as governor. In his address given on January 6, 1829, Van Buren mentioned the state road, the Chenango Canal, and the Chemung Canal as internal improvements that should be commenced. He pointed out that many areas across the state had supported and helped pay for the Erie and Champlain canals. Now, those areas should be rewarded with improvements that more directly benefited their regions.[54]

Chemung Canal backers hoped that having an ally in a governor, who supported internal improvements, would help their chances, and they hoped to get the bill before the legislature as soon as possible.[55] Unfortunately, most New Yorkers knew Van Buren would not warm the governor's seat for long. Andrew Jackson, the newly elected president, made it clear he would nominate Van Buren to serve as secretary of state. By March 1829, Van Buren had left for Washington, and Lieutenant Governor Enos Throop ascended to the governor's chair.

Throop was not as friendly to canals as Van Buren was. He believed railroads were the future of American transportation. While in the senate as lieuten-

51 *Geneva Gazette and General Advertiser*, April 23, 1828, p. 3.
52 Ibid., June 11, 1828, p. 3.
53 Ibid., December 24, 1828, p. 3; January 21, 1829, p. 3; February 4, 1829, p. 3.
54 "Governor's Message," *Albany Argus*, January 7, 1829, p. 2.
55 *Geneva Gazette and General Advertiser*, December 10, 1828, p. 3.

ant governor, Throop had opposed the Chenango Canal bill because he preferred to see a railroad built in its place.[56] It would be helpful that Throop was no longer in the senate to lead any possible opposition to the bill, but if the bill reached the governor's desk, would he sign it? That question was not the only worry facing advocates of the Chemung Canal.

A chief concern lay in the potential for another canal proposal to sway attention from the Chemung Canal if it could prove more expedient. Residents in Steuben and Yates counties began endorsing a plan that originally called for a canal from Bath to Keuka Lake and from there to Seneca Lake. This canal, known as the Crooked Lake Canal, would later be revised to simply connect Keuka (Crooked) Lake to Seneca Lake, making it only eight miles long. The Crooked Lake Canal could be a more attractive project if it could be built more cheaply than the Chemung Canal. Those allied to the Chemung Canal resented this local competition after working so long and getting so close to seeing the bill passed. The Crooked Lake Canal would have to wait its turn. Little did they realize that the two canals would eventually pass the legislature in the same year and be constructed at the same time.

The *Geneva Gazette and General Advertiser* pointed out the advantages the Chemung Canal would have over the Crooked Lake Canal. The Chemung Canal would give easier access to the Pennsylvania coal fields, a commodity that was much needed; the Crooked Lake Canal would not. The Chemung Canal, though longer, would actually be cheaper to build since the terrain it would traverse was not as steep as the route proposed for the Crooked Lake Canal. Plans estimated the Chemung Canal would require 44 locks and that 66 would be needed on the Crooked Lake Canal. If one had to choose between these two routes, it appeared that the Chemung Canal was the logical choice.[57]

Another public work being considered proposed building a railroad from Havana (Montour Falls) to the Chemung River. Boats could travel from Seneca Lake to Havana using Catharine Creek. The village planned to ask the legislature to incorporate a company to build a railroad to Elmira and also to improve the inlet to the lake to allow steamboats to travel on it. Goods could be transshipped from the railroad to canal boats and then towed by steamboat to Geneva and the Seneca and Cayuga Canal.[58] If such a scheme proved practical, the chances for the Chemung Canal would be sunk.

Fortunately for the Chemung Canal, two other projects began moving forward that made building the Chemung Canal a more attractive idea. The Cayuga

56 Ray Smith, *Political and Governmental History of the State of New York* (Syracuse, N.Y.: Syracuse Press, 1922), pp. 124–5.
57 *Geneva Gazette and General Advertiser*, December 10, 1828, p. 3. The original proposal for the Crooked Lake Canal called for a canal from Bath, N.Y., to Crooked Lake (Keuka) and then from Penn Yan on Crooked Lake to the town of Dresden on Seneca Lake. Such a canal would have been 14 miles long and would have necessitated 66 locks. The final canal was actually from Penn Yan to Dresden, a distance of 8 miles requiring 28 locks.
58 Ibid., January 26, 1829, p. 3.

and Seneca Canal, which had been authorized by the legislature in 1825, opened in November 1828.[59] The Cayuga and Seneca Canal allowed direct access to the Erie Canal from the northern end of Seneca Lake. Connecting the southern end of Seneca Lake to the Chemung River would extend inland water navigation and include a larger region in a market exchange. The Chemung Canal would make both the Cayuga and Seneca Canal and the Erie more profitable by opening up a whole new southern region to them, thus increasing traffic and tolls.

The Pennsylvania Canal gained approval from the Pennsylvania legislature in 1829 with plans to eventually connect Harrisburg to Tioga Point on the Susquehanna River at Athens, Pennsylvania. With Athens only a short distance from Corning, where the feeder to the proposed Chemung Canal would begin, many people in New York and Pennsylvania speculated about eventually extending the Chemung Canal to join the Pennsylvania Canal. By adding a railroad that could bring coal directly from the mines in Pennsylvania to the canals, the two canals could become important means for supplying a large region with abundant coal.[60]

The chance for success burned brighter as the battle in the legislature for the Chemung Canal began again in January 1829. On January 23, the assembly received a petition asking the legislature to authorize the Chemung Canal. It was followed by another on February 6. The assembly heard a very favorable report on the Chemung Canal given by Benjamin P. Johnson from Oneida, the canal committee chairman. Johnson then introduced the bill to the assembly. By March 27, the assembly was ready to consider the Chemung Canal bill.[61]

Johnson addressed the assembly on the merits offered by the Chemung Canal bill. Relying on the figures compiled by the late Dugald Cameron, Johnson argued that the Chemung Canal's expense would be more than offset by the increased trade it would stimulate. The difficult and risky navigation on the Susquehanna River would assure a steady traffic in lumber, grain, meat, and coal to New York markets through the safer Chemung and Erie Canals. Johnson attempted to placate those worried about excessive construction costs by offering an amendment to the bill, capping the construction expense at $300,000. It also provided that work should not begin on the canal until the canal commissioners had made all the contracts necessary to insure its completion.[62] Johnson argued that the abundant wealth to be gained from such a small expense made the Chemung Canal an obvious and logical step in extending the internal improvements that had already yielded great economic benefits for New York State. Johnson's home district witnessed the tremendous impact the Erie Canal had on

59 Ibid., April 29, 1829, p. 3; *The Cayuga and Seneca Canal*, http://www.history.rochester.edu/canal/bib/whitford/old 1906/chapter8.htm. Accessed March 2000.
60 *Geneva Gazette and General Advertiser*, April 29, 1829, p. 3.
61 *Albany Argus*, January 24, 1829, p. 2; February 5, 1829, p. 2; February 7, 1829, p. 2; March 28, 1829, p. 2; *Geneva Gazette and General Advertiser*, February 11, 1829.
62 *Albany Argus*, March 2, 1829, p. 2; March 31, 1829, p. 2; "Chemung Canal Report," *Geneva Gazette and General Advertiser*, February 18, 1829, p. 2.

No. 66.

In Assembly,

February 4, 1829.

[Brought in by Mr. JOHNSON.]

AN ACT

Authorising the construction of a canal from the head of Seneca lake to Newtown.

The People of the State of New-York, represented in Senate and Assembly, do enact as follows:

1 § 1. The canal commissioners are hereby authorised and required to
2 proceed with all practicable diligence, to construct and complete a naviga-
3 ble canal from the head waters of the Seneca lake, to the Chemung river,
4 (a branch of the Susquehannah,) at the village of Newtown, in the county of
5 Tioga, with a navigable feeder from the Chimney Narrows to the summit
6 level of said canal, in such manner as the said commissioners may deem most
7 advisable and best calculated to promote the interests of this state and the
8 public convenience; and for the accomplishment of the work, and the re-
9 gulation and use of the same, and collecting the tolls thereon, the like pow-
10 ers are hereby conferred on and extended to the canal commissioners and
11 the canal board, as they have possessed or now possess under the several
12 laws of this state, relating to the Erie and Champlain canals.

1 § 2. The commissioners of the canal fund shall be, and they are hereby
2 authorised and directed to borrow, from time to time, on the credit of the
3 state, at an interest not exceeding five per centum per annum, such sum or
4 sums of money as shall be necessary to construct and complete the said ca-
5 nal and feeder, in amount not exceeding three hundred thousand dollars,
6 for which monies so to be borrowed, certificates of stock shall be issued in
7 the manner directed in and by the act, entitled "an act to improve the funds
8 and to provide for the redemption of the funded debt of this state," and to
9 pay the monies so to be borrowed to the canal commissioners, to be applied
10 in the construction of the aforesaid work.

1 § 3. No monies shall be borrowed by virtue of this act, and the construct-
2 ing said canal shall not be commenced, until the Seneca and Susquehannah
3 Lock Navigation Company, incorporated by an act passed March 31, 1815,
4 entitled "an act for opening the navigation between the head waters of the
5 Seneca lake and the Chemung river," shall have released to and vested in
6 the people of this state, all the rights, powers, privileges and immunities
7 granted by the said act to the said company.

The New York State Assembly passed the bill to build the Chemung Canal in 1829. The senate also approved the bill, which finally paved the way for the canal to become a reality after several failures to get the bill passed. The Chemung County Historical Society has an original copy of the bill. (The Booth Library of the Chemung County Historical Society)

Rome, and Johnson knew that having lateral canals feeding into the Erie would assure continued growth.

On March 30 Amasa Dana from Ithaca spoke against the bill for nearly an hour. Dana's speech had little effect as the assembly voted to accept Johnson's amendment and then passed the bill with a 75 to 31 majority.[63]

Gratton Wheeler from Bath stood among those who had voted against the bill. In January, as the legislature just opened its business for the 1829 session, a Bath, New York, resident sent a letter addressed to Wheeler and Senator Morris Sheppard from Penn Yan. The letter gave a testimonial favoring the Crooked Lake Canal and expounded nearly all the same arguments that had been relied upon to justify the Chemung Canal. Both men voted against the Chemung Canal in their respective houses. It was clear that local competition for canal routes was an impediment that threatened the Chemung Canal, but the vote in the assembly showed that many representatives realized that the best way to get votes for their local projects would be to support those in nearby regions. With the assembly voicing such clear support for the Chemung Canal, perhaps the senate would finally endorse the project.

Senator Thomas Waterman introduced the Chemung Canal bill in the senate on Wednesday, April 8, and it became the special order for that Saturday. At the Saturday session, the senate convened to discuss the bill. The assembly canal committee report from Mr. Johnson was read, followed by a petition from a meeting in Elmira requesting the senate to pass the bill. Other readings included information about the recent survey conducted by the Army and the senate canal committee report from 1827.

The most vocal objection to the Chemung Canal in the senate came from Senator Walker Todd, representing the second senate district near New York City. Senator Todd made a motion that the bill be amended to exclude building the canal from Horseheads to Elmira. Todd claimed that section only served some narrow interest in Elmira. Where was the public benefit if the canal terminated in Elmira with nowhere else to go? He opposed spending public monies to benefit only one community. His amendment would save money by having the canal constructed only from Seneca Lake to the junction with the feeder canal at Horseheads. Access to the Chemung River could be attained through the feeder canal. The senate discussed Todd's amendment and then voted it down.[64]

Senator Todd resumed his opposition to the Chemung Canal on Monday, April 13. He spoke at length about his objections to the bill. Todd doubted that the estimates for building the Chemung Canal were accurate. Estimated to cost less than $12,000 per mile to build, the Chemung Canal would be exceptionally cheap compared to other canals that had been completed. Todd said that actual construction costs almost always soared to levels above estimates due to unfore-

63 *Albany Argus*, March 31, 1829, p. 2; April 1, 1829, p. 2.
64 Ibid., April 13, 1829, p. 2; May 1, 1829, p. 2.

seen complications. The Delaware and Hudson Canal had cost over $16,000 per mile to construct, and that had been considered a canal built with great prudence and efficiency.

Todd also questioned the figures used to show the revenue that the Chemung Canal would contribute. Since the Chenango Canal had been approved to be built, and it too would connect the Erie Canal to the Susquehanna River, would not coal shipments be sent on both the Chemung and the Chenango? Also, what if other public projects such as the Pennsylvania Canal's North Branch were never completed? How would the coal get to the canals? The estimates that counted on the Chemung Canal to ship large quantities of coal might not come to pass, and the tolls collected could be far less than expected. If that happened, the canal would not pay for itself as promised, and the taxpayers would shoulder the burden to pay off the debt incurred by building the canal.[65]

In the afternoon session on April 13, Charles Stebbins, the new lieutenant governor, sought to amend the Chemung Canal bill to include a stipulation that the work could not exceed $300,000. Like Todd, Stebbins questioned the earlier Chemung Canal surveys and the estimates for its costs and revenues. Stebbins believed another survey would verify that the canal could not be built at the actual projected cost. His suggestion received little support since others objected that enough surveys and estimates had been done. It made no sense to do another.[66]

On Tuesday, April 14, the Chemung Canal bill was given its third reading before the senate in preparation for the final vote. The opposition made one last effort to stop its progress. A question arose whether the bill was a two-thirds or a majority bill. The president of the senate decided it was a procedural question and ruled that the bill was a two-thirds bill. After much discussion, it was moved by Senator Peter Hager from Ithaca that it be a majority bill, and the motion carried.

The next obstacle involved the corporate charter that created the Seneca and Susquehannah Lock Navigation Company. The Chemung Canal bill stipulated that no money should be borrowed to build the canal, and construction should not commence until the Seneca and Susquehannah Lock Navigation Company relinquished its rights to construct the canal. This point proved moot when Senator Thomas Waterman pointed out that the company had forfeited its rights under the terms in the original charter. The charter granted by the state legislature included a clause specifying that unless the company began constructing the canal within 14 years it would lose its corporate rights. The clock had run out on the Seneca and Susquehannah Lock Navigation Company on March 31, 1828.[67]

The clock also ran out on those senators opposed to the Chemung Canal. There would be no more stalling. The final roll call vote showed that eighteen senators voted for the canal, and seven voted against it. The bill had finally cleared

65 Ibid., May 1, 1829, p. 2.
66 Ibid., April 14, 1829, p. 2.
67 Ibid., April 15, 1829, p. 2.

the senate. Governor Throop made it a law by signing the bill just a few days later.[68]

The news touched off exuberant celebrations in Elmira and Geneva. Genevans celebrated the good news with cannon fire, and the steamboat waiting to ferry passengers to Jefferson rang its bell loudly. A music professor from West Point who was visiting Geneva at the time composed a piece called "The Chemung Canal Grand March" and performed it at a concert.[69] Elmira farmers, upon hearing bells ringing and cannons firing, headed into Elmira to join the celebration. In both Geneva and Elmira a great deal of drinking accompanied the merriment. One witness at the Elmira jubilation reported that the "whole town was drunk."[70]

On May 8 Elmira hosted a more formal victory celebration. Many men were absent when the news arrived because they had traveled down the Susquehanna River to take their produce to market. With their return, an elaborate dinner was planned. The dinner was held at the Mansion House, a tavern run by "Judge" Bundy. The household was highly decorated with flags and banners. A special flag was made just for the occasion. It had 18 stars on one side and the words "Chemung Canal." On the other side was inscribed "Gratitude, 15th April, 1829."[71]

The dinner was presided over by Solomon L. Smith, and he was assisted by Major Lyman Covell and Thomas Maxwell. Between the cannon blasts and the loud cheers, a great many toasts were offered, paying tribute to the men and communities who had made their vision become reality.

Francis Granger, B. P. Johnson, the late Dugald Cameron, and Frederic and William DeZeng were among the men who were saluted for their roles in getting the Chemung Canal bill passed. The toasts also recognized the surrounding communities that helped the cause. Geneva received particular attention for the great effort its citizens contributed, and Ontario County was saluted for furnishing "more advocates for the Chemung Canal, both in and out of the legislature, than any other county in the state." William Dunn gave the final toast. He said: "Our aged and patriotic guest, Col. John Hendy—Who first broke ground and raised potatoes in the old town of Newtown—May he be the first to break ground on the summit level of the Chemung Canal."[72]

A year later, on the Fourth of July, Hendy was the first to break ground for the canal. As a crowd watched, he stood in a small boat on the Chemung River

68 Ibid., April 15, 1829, p. 2; *Geneva Gazette and General Advertiser*, April 22, 1829, p. 2; *Geneva Gazette and General Advertiser*, April 29, 1829, excerpt from the *Ovid Free Press*, p. 3.

69 *Geneva Gazette and General Advertiser*, April 22, 1829, p. 3; April 29, 1829, p. 3.

70 Ibid., April 29, 1829, excerpt from the *Elmira Gazette* and the *Ovid Free Press*, p. 3; *Ithaca Journal*, April 29, 1829, p. 3; Towner, *A History of the Valley and County of Chemung*, 124–5.

71 *Geneva Gazette and General Advertiser*, May 27, 1829, p. 1; Towner, *A History of the Valley and County of Chemung*, 136.

72 *Geneva Gazette and General Advertiser*, May 27, 1829, p. 1.

bank and turned the first shovelful of earth. Twelve other early pioneers from the area joined in with picks, shovels, and wheelbarrows to contribute their part to the ceremony. James Robinson, a local justice of the peace, then made a speech that outlined the great effort by the many people who had made the Chemung Canal possible. He concluded with a tribute to the late Andrew McNab from Geneva, who had done so much to secure the bill's passage.

The crowd then moved to the Presbyterian Church, where they sang:

> Day of glory, welcome day;
> Freedom's banners greet thy ray;
> See how cheerfully they play
> In the morning breeze.
>
> On the heights where patriots kneeled;
> On the plains where squadrons wheeled;
> When a tyrant's thunder pealed
> O'er our trembling seas.[73]

---

73 *Elmira Sunday Telegram*, July 5, 1885, reprinted in "Ground Breaking for Canal 'Great Day' in 1830," *The Chemung Historical Journal*, vol. 1, no. 4 (June 1956): 166; Towner, *A History of the Valley and County of Chemung*, 125; *Geneva Gazette and Mercantile Advertiser*, July 21, 1830, p. 3.

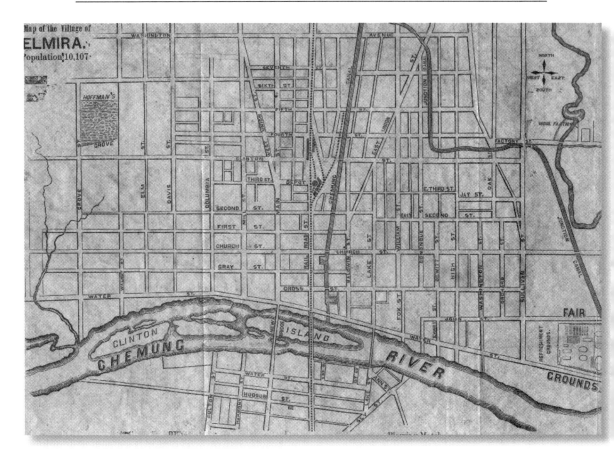

This 1855 map of Elmira shows the route of the Chemung Canal through the city. When the canal was later closed and filled in, the old canal route became State Street. State Street was later replaced by the Clemens Center Parkway. (The Booth Library of the Chemung County Historical Society)

CHAPTER TWO

PROCEED WITH THE
Construction of the Work

THE BATTLE TO PASS THE CHEMUNG CANAL BILL had been won; now began the battle to build it. Building the canal would not be the easy task that early speculation made it appear. Topography, labor problems, politics, and flooding all contributed to delaying completion. The construction, which engineers projected would take two years, took over three years to complete.

The topography posed some difficult obstacles. The land rose over 400 feet from Seneca Lake to Horseheads. That meant building many locks within a short distance. The canal and the feeder had 51 locks altogether, and 40 were between Horseheads and Jefferson (Watkins Glen). In comparison, the Erie Canal had 83 locks on its 363 mile course.[1] Having so many locks increased the construction expense and meant higher operating costs as many lock tenders would be required to operate the locks. It was decided to use wooden locks rather than stone to save money. Although that decision helped to keep costs down and secure approval for the canal, in the long run it proved unwise. The wooden locks lacked durability and contributed to the canal's short history.

The sandy soil along the canal route made for easy digging, but it easily caved in, making the digging dangerous. The porous soil allowed water to leak from the canal, and canal banks easily broke during flooding. Many streams crossed the terrain, and the canal often ran alongside them. Every flood brought damage to the canal that required expensive repairs.

The contract system used to solicit bids to build the canal contained inherent problems that slowed construction. The system did not allow for unexpected difficulties, and it encouraged practices that led to improper work and forfeited contracts. The ones who suffered most were the workers, mainly Irish immi-

---

1 Sheriff, *The Artificial River*, p. 30.

grants, who labored under conditions that included low pay and poor housing. They were sometimes left unpaid by the contractors. Crime, alcohol abuse, and disease thrived among them.

A political threat almost put an end to the canal even before construction began. Not all the canal commissioners favored the Chemung Canal. Commissioner Samuel Young voiced his opposition to the state assembly. In an unusual move, Young refused to sign the annual report submitted by the other two canal commissioners, Henry Seymour and William Bouck, and submitted his own report. Young believed that the estimates for the revenues to be realized from the Chemung Canal were greatly exaggerated. He feared the canal would not pay for its expenses and would, therefore, cost the taxpayers more money. In fact, the canal commissioners had reported on February 5, 1830, that the tolls collected from the Chemung and Crooked Lake Canals would not be sufficient to defray the interest on the loans or the expense for repairs.

Young warned that the many lateral canals being proposed would saddle the state with a large amount of debt. The end result would be "heavy debt, grievous taxation, waning finances, depressed trade, depopulated cities, and an alienated people."[2] Young, from Saratoga County, was voicing his displeasure at financing so many internal improvements that would not benefit his county, but he also showed concern for taxpayers across the state. The cost of building and maintaining so many canals could saddle the taxpayers with a heavy debt.

The assembly passed a resolution directing the canal commissioners to send the legislature a report citing the projected costs and revenues for the Chemung and Crooked Lake Canals. In the assembly the assault on the Chemung Canal was led by its old nemesis, Abijah Mann Jr. from Herkimer County, and his new ally from Tompkins County, Jonathan Gosman. Mann and Gosman introduced resolutions to suspend Chemung Canal construction until the legislature gave further directions to the canal commissioners. Mann rose in the assembly to defend his resolution but was too ill to finish. The assembly postponed the decision for a week to allow Mann to recover his health.

Those supporting the Chemung Canal realized they could not afford to lose any more time. Many other important bills sought assembly approval. The Chenango Canal awaited consideration, and many banks were seeking incorporation. If the delay continued much longer, the Chemung Canal could be pushed aside and left on hold until the following year.

Mann tried to delay as much as possible, but the Chemung Canal backers would not be denied. They aggressively insisted that the resolution be brought before the assembly, discussed, and voted on. On April 7, 1830, Assemblyman Andrew Dickinson from Steuben County called for a vote on Mann's resolution in an attempt to settle the question. Mann once again cited his illness when request-

2 New York State Assembly, Legislative Document no.195, February 23, 1830, New York State Library; *Albany Argus*, March 19, 1830, pp. 1–2; *Ithaca Journal*, February 10, 1830, p. 2.

ing that the measure be left on the table. Dickinson would not hear it. Allied with powerful Francis Granger from Ontario County and Luther Bradish from Franklin County, Dickinson demanded the question be resolved. Further delay would be unfair to the local citizens affected by the improvement and those who had made contracts to do the work. They should not be kept in suspense any longer. Mann's request to postpone the debate on the resolution was put to a vote and lost.[3]

Tioga County's representative, John G. McDowell, took the floor to defend the canal that promised to transform his home district. That the Chemung Canal issue came at a time when so many other crucial issues pressed upon the lawmakers should not be blamed on the Chemung Canal supporters, McDowell explained. He had done all he could to get the issue before the assembly before the other legislation came up on the calendar but faced delays due to Mann's illness and the six-week wait for the canal commissioners' report from the canal committee. McDowell had even promised Mann he would wait two weeks to allow Mann to recover his health and prepare his speeches. The time for being gracious was over. It was time to act.

Mann continued his attempt to delay the decision only to be overwhelmed by those favoring the Chemung Canal. When the final vote on his resolution was counted, 75 voted against it, and only 35 voted for it.[4] The legislature had reaffirmed its support for the Chemung Canal. The contracts had been let, and the workmen were ready to begin. On June 11, 1830, Canal Commissioners William Bouck and Henry Seymour wrote to the commissioners of the canal funds:

> Contracts for the construction of the Chemung Canal having been obtained for a Sum not exceeding two hundred and eighty two thousand dollars with ample built in for their performance . . . we believe the conditions required by the law authorizing this canal have been complied with, and we conceive it to be our duty to proceed with the construction of the work.[5]

The work could finally begin. To finance the construction, $150,000 needed to be borrowed for the first six months of work. The comptroller advertised for bids to raise the money and obtained the loan by July.[6] Elmira had already held its ground-breaking ceremony, and gangs were busy working all along the canal. Work progressed quickly. The *Elmira Gazette* reported by late August that a half-mile stretch near Horseheads was near completion. Workmen filled that section

---

3 *Albany Argus*, March 27, 1830, excerpt from the *Assembly Journal*, p. 2; April 2, 1830, p. 2; April 9, 1830, p. 2.
4 *Albany Argus*, April 2, 1830, p. 2; April 9, 1830, p. 2; *Geneva Gazette and Mercantile Advertiser*, April 14, 1830, p. 3.
5 William Bouck and Henry Seymour to the commissioners of the canal funds, June 11, 1830, William Bouck Papers, Cornell University.
6 Ibid.; *Geneva Gazette* and *General Advertiser*, June 16, 1830, p. 3; July 28, 1830, p. 3.

The Elmira Gazette reported on the progress of the Chemung Canal shortly after construction began in 1830. (Elmira Gazette, Steele Memorial Library)

with water but only to provide amusement for the local people. Charles Dunn began offering rides on the two-mile section in September for twenty-five cents.[7]

Although the work began smoothly, the topography yielded difficulties that slowed the work. Holmes Hutchinson served as the chief engineer to oversee the Chemung Canal construction. He gained experience helping to build the Erie Canal and eventually served as the chief engineer for the Erie Canal from 1835 to 1841.[8] Hutchinson surveyed the Chemung Canal route to see what the work would entail. He completed his survey by September 9, 1829, and wrote his report to the canal commissioners.

7   *Elmira Gazette*, August 28, 1830, p. 2; September 10, 1831, p. 3.
8   Whitford, *History of the Canal System*, p. 1157.

Hutchinson reported that the feeder canal would join the main canal at the summit level at Horseheads. Horseheads stood only 47 feet higher in elevation than Elmira but loomed 441 feet higher in elevation than Seneca Lake. Most locks on the canal would be needed between the lake and Horseheads. Hutchinson estimated that 53 locks would be needed. Each lock would be 90 feet long, 15 feet wide, and 10 feet high. At $2,000 each they would be the most expensive feature.

The canal prism would be 42 feet across at the surface, 26 feet across at the base, and 4 feet deep. Hutchinson estimated that the cost to dig the canal prism and build a towpath would be $5,000 per mile. With 39 miles to dig, this would amount to $195,000. Hutchinson believed that most digging would not be difficult. North from Elmira lay a large swamp. There the canal banks would have to be supported with wooden walls. At various points along the route, shafts had been dug to determine the soil composition.[9] Beyond the swamp areas and along the feeder route the soil tests showed the soil to be mainly sand, loam, and gravel, which made for easy excavation. The workers used primarily pick and shovel, but newer technology did provide some assistance. Two mechanical stump extractors were used to grub the canal path. Hutchinson reported that one machine removed 211 stumps in one day on section 11.[10]

Although the sandy soil made the excavation easier, it also made it dangerous. Digging in the Millport area proved especially hazardous. There the canal

While the Chemung Canal was being constructed, Charles Dunn of Horseheads charged local people 25 cents for the chance to take a boat ride on a complete portion of the canal. (Elmira Gazette, September 10, 1831, p. 3)

9   Ibid., pp. 613, 617; *Geneva Gazette and Mercantile Advertiser*, September 16, 1829, p. 3.
10 *Elmira Gazette*, August 20, 1831, p. 2.

snaked its way along sandy hillsides deposited by the glaciers. The soil easily gave way, creating landslides. On December 8, 1830, a high embankment collapsed onto some workers digging at its base, killing three men and injuring two. Due to the soil composition in many places along the route, landslides were a problem throughout the canal's construction.[11]

As the canal digging approached Havana, workers made a surprising discovery. The canal had been surveyed to run through a Seneca Indian cemetery. Many bodies were disinterred by workers digging near the site that had been Catharine's Town, which had been destroyed by the Sullivan and Clinton campaign during the Revolutionary War. Queen Catharine Montour, a woman of French, Huron, and Seneca descent, and the other villagers had fled the advancing army. Now the Chemung Canal had arrived to disturb those Senecas left to rest in peace in the former Indian village. The workers moved the graves to a small hill nearby. Later, Charles Cook created a cemetery there. The Cook family plot and a few other forgotten graves can still be seen on the hill near B. C. Cate Elementary School in Montour Falls. A monument to Queen Catharine is also there.[12]

Another obstacle encountered when building the Chemung Canal was the deep cut in Big Flats. The feeder canal crossed Big Flats to bring water to the canal at Horseheads. The canal bed had to be dug as deep as 20 feet in places to supply water in an uninterrupted flow from the Chemung feeder dam at Gibson to Horseheads. Luke Hitchcock, who had been a contractor on the Erie Canal, elected to tackle the deep cut and found his new task a formidable one. The path for the deep cut had to be moved shortly after beginning work. The new line crossed a heavily wooded area that had to be cleared. It also crossed Sing Sing Creek. As the crew dug, they encountered water that had to be constantly bailed out. They worked in the cold water and mud. Horses got stuck and became useless. The workers had to resort to wheelbarrows to conduct the excavation. Hitchcock said it "was unquestionably the worst excavation that we have ever seen on any canal."[13] Engineer Joseph Dana Allen agreed with the assessment. Hitchcock later petitioned the legislature to be given an extra allowance on his contract since the job had been changed after he made his bid.[14]

The many streams that crisscrossed the landscape presented another challenge. It would be too expensive to build many aqueducts to carry the canal over the streams. It made more sense to move the streams. In some places, Newtown Creek, Sing Sing Creek, and Catharine Creek had to be altered from their natural courses to accommodate the canal. The streams running alongside the canal

11 *Geneva Gazette and General Advertiser*, December 22, 1830, excerpt from the *Elmira Gazette*, p. 3; Holmes Hutchinson to William Bouck, August 16, 1832, William Bouck Papers, Cornell University.

12 Carl B. Garey, *Legacies from Queen Catharine Montour and Charles Cook: A History of Montour and Montour Falls, New York* (1974), Montour Falls Memorial Library.

13 Petition of Luke Hitchcock and Company to the Canal Board of New York State, April 18, 1833, and Deposition by Joseph Dana Allen to the Canal Board, April 19, 1833, Series A1140, 1833, Packets 26 and 27, New York State Archives; Craig Williams, *Field Trip Guide, October 31, 1998: The Chemung Canal*, The Canal Society of New York State, p. 20.

14 Ibid.

would necessitate many expensive repairs in the future due to the flooding that occurred nearly every year. The fast moving water often cut into the prism, washing in gravel and sweeping away towpaths.[15]

Supplying the canal with sufficient water meant harnessing the Chemung River. Plans called for a dam at Gibson near Corning to fulfill the task. Situated at a site known as Chimney Rocks for the unusual rock formation there, the feeder dam created a large pool that supplied most of the water for the Chemung Canal. The 7-foot-high and 645-foot-wide wooden dam included a chute to allow timber rafts to pass by and continue on to the Susquehanna River. Raftsmen considered it a nuisance and sometimes attempted to dismantle it. The chute often made their journey more dangerous as the sudden drop into deep water broke apart heavily loaded rafts.[16] However, the Chemung River often did its best to oblige the raftsmen and sweep away the man-made impediment within its stream, making the dam a source of frequent expense when flood waters tore sections apart and undermined its supports.

The landscape had been expected to present difficulties and delays, but work on the canal also slowed due to another unforeseen problem. The system used to let the contracts for the Chemung Canal contained inherent weaknesses that resulted in abandoned contracts and labor shortages.

In November 1829 newspaper advertisements solicited bids from contractors to build the Chemung Canal. The canal commissioners divided the canal route into 35 sections, with separate contracts being accepted for each section. The advertisement called for bids from contractors to build 53 locks, 3 aqueducts, 6 culverts, 70 bridges, the feeder dam, and one stone guard lock. All the sealed bids were to be received by the canal commissioners by January 1, 1830. Hutchinson made himself available along the canal route in mid-December to show construction plans and to furnish forms for making bids.[17]

Charles Cook, a prominent businessman from Havana (Montour Falls), formed a company along with Samuel Farwell and George Spencer. They contracted to build many sections of the canal and received the contracts to build sections 1, 2, 5, 11, and sections 28 through 35. Their company also won the contracts to build all the aqueducts, culverts, waste weirs, and lockhouses. To complete so many varied tasks necessitated hiring subcontractors who had experience building canals. Asa Cady, who had built many aqueducts on the Erie Canal, was brought in to oversee the aqueduct construction on the Chemung Canal.

Five separate contracts were let to build the locks. Each winning bid received approximately 10 locks to build. Like the aqueducts, nonlocal men with

---

15 "Report of Holmes Hutchinson, Engineer, in relation to the construction of the Chemung and Crooked Lake Canals," Canal Commissioners Papers, New York State Library; *Geneva Gazette and Mercantile Advertiser*, September 16, 1829, p. 3.

16 Thomas Dimitroff and Lois Janes, *History of the Corning-Painted Post Area* (Corning, New York: Corning Area Bicentennial Committee, 1977), p. 24, p. 27; Whitford, *History of the Canal System*, p. 618, p. 621.

17 *Geneva Gazette and General Advertiser*, November 25, 1829, p. 3; Chemung Canal Contracts, Packet 1, Series A1189, New York State Archives; Dimitroff and Janes, *History of the Corning-Painted Post Area*, p. 24.

Charles Cook arrived in Havana (Montour Falls) in 1829 to help build the Chemung Canal. Together with some other men, he formed the company Spencer, Farwell, Cook and Company. This company contracted to build many sections of the Chemung Canal, and they built most of the lockkeepers' houses. Cook was a tremendous benefactor to his adopted town of Havana. He opened many enterprises along the canal in the town including sawmills, a flour mill, and a coal yard. He built the Montour House, St. Paul's Episcopal Church, People's College, and the Bank of Havana, all of which still stand in Montour Falls. Today, the bank is the Montour Falls Memorial Library. Cook secured a land grant under the Morrill Act for his People's College, only to later lose it to Ezra Cornell in Ithaca. Cook helped to create Schuyler County and hoped to make his town the county seat. He even built a courthouse, sheriff's office, and a jail in anticipation of his success. Unfortunately, in a hotly contested battle, he lost his quest for the county seat to Watkins Glen. While Cook built his fortune around the canal, he added to his wealth by contracting to build part of the Erie Railroad. He was an active politician as well. Cook served as one of the canal commissioners in the early 1850s and was elected to the New York State Senate in 1863. Shortly after his election, he suffered a stroke; a second stroke in 1866 proved fatal. He is buried in Cook Cemetery in Montour Falls alongside the former route of the Chemung Canal. The cemetery can be reached via the Queen Catharine Trail in Montour Falls. (Montour Falls Memorial Library)

experience were relied upon to provide their expertise in constructing the locks. Luke Hitchcock from Madison County and Caleb Hammel from Rome, who had both worked on the Erie Canal, joined in partnership with some local men to build many of the Chemung Canal locks.[18]

The contract system served as the typical arrangement for building canals during this time, but it included intrinsic problems that slowed progress on the Chemung Canal. Contractors had to state the cost for various tasks they would be required to do such as grubbing and clearing, excavation, and masonry, but the contract allowed little room for unforeseen difficulties that could cause the job to exceed the original bid. The lowest bid got the job, so contractors had to keep their costs as low as possible if they wished to get the work, which often proved detrimental to the workers the contractors hired. Since the contractor was responsible for housing and feeding his employees, the temptation was there to cut costs by supplying inadequate room and board. The contractor intended to make a profit, even if it meant creating miserable conditions for the workers.

Subcontracting, later banned on many canal contracts in other states due to the problems it created, flourished on the Chemung Canal. Since the contractor insisted on protecting his profit, subcontractors had to do the job at a cost even lower than what the contractor had bid. In their haste to get work, subcontractors often made unrealistic bids that left them with no hope of earning a profit for themselves. Faced with mounting costs and bound to a contract, subcontractors frequently had to stop work when they ran out of money. Some just abandoned their contracts. Of course the last to be paid were the workers, who often found there was no money left over for them.[19]

Work on the Chemung Canal slowed to a crawl in 1832 because of the subcontractors. The canal commissioners' report about the Chemung Canal's progress during 1831 stated that many subcontractors "were men possessing neither character nor responsibility."[20] Numerous subcontractors had bid far too low on their jobs. As a result, the commissioners reported that many workers left the canal unpaid and disgusted.

Millport citizens especially suffered due to the negligent subcontractors. Many merchants and farmers around Millport had extended credit to subcontractors for supplies, only to lose their money when the work stopped.[21] The subcontractors had no money left to pay their creditors. Local residents figured the canal would make them wealthy; instead, it appeared to be draining their wealth away.

The situation also drained away labor. With so many canals being constructed at once, contractors found it difficult to keep an adequate work force.

18 Chemung Canal Contracts, Packet 1, New York State Archives; Williams, Field Trip Guide, p. 5.
19 Peter Way, *Common Labor: Workers and the Digging of North American Canals* (New York: Cambridge University Press, 1993), pp. 59–68.
20 *Annual Report of the Canal Commissioners*, 1832, p. 13, New York State Archives.
21 Richard Wich, "Millport Named for 17 Mills of Canal," undated newspaper article in "Canals" folder, Chemung County Historical Society.

Besides the Chemung Canal, the Crooked Lake Canal and the Pennsylvania Canal had also begun construction. When canal workers had a choice, they chose the work site that had little disease, good pay, and a reliable employer who paid his workers.[22] Faced with irresponsible subcontractors on the Chemung Canal, many workers voted with their feet and left for better opportunities. The labor shortage that resulted increased construction expenses by driving up wages.[23]

By 1832, Holmes Hutchinson and fellow engineer Joseph Dana Allen complained to the canal commissioners about the slow progress being made due to a labor shortage. Allen reported in May 1832 that sections 16 and 17 on the Chemung Canal were moving very slowly since the contractors only had 12 to 16 men in their employ, with little hope for getting more. By August the situation had improved only slightly. Allen wrote to canal commissioner William Bouck:

> Sections 16 & 17 of the Smith and Baldwin jobs are progress-ing as fast as 30 to 35 men can advance with them. Labor is scarce and we are unable to drive it at this time faster than it is now progressing. A new force was organized upon the work immediately after you left us, under the charge of William Newton, and it will probably require another month to complete the two sections, and perhaps a little longer.[24]

The contractors and subcontractors had a different perspective on the matter. They argued the blame lay with the state government. They relied on the state to provide them with prompt payment as the work progressed to cover their expenses. Delays in getting the cash they desperately needed created huge headaches. Letters from Holmes Hutchinson to canal commissioner William Bouck included passages about the need to pay contractors who were in dire need. Hutchinson warned the canal commissioners in 1831 that "punctuality in the pay-ments to the contractors is of importance, particularly as the greatest proportion of work is subcontracted and done by persons who are wholly made to perform their work without frequent and liberal payments."[25] In July 1832 Hutchinson wrote to Bouck that contractor Charles Cook "stated that he was out of funds. His men had not been paid and that . . . he must have cash or stop the work."[26] A month later, Cook still anxiously awaited his money.

Sometimes payments to the contractors were delayed due to the engineer. The engineer and the contractor could find themselves at odds with one another because each had a different goal. The engineer worked for the state. He had an

22 Way, *Common Labor*, pp. 120–22; Catherine Tobin, "Irish Labor on American Canals," *Canal History and Technology Proceedings* (March 17, 1990): pp. 169–70.
23 *Annual Report of the Canal Commissioners*, 1833, p. 4.
24 Joseph Dana Allen to William Bouck, May 30, 1832 and August 12, 1832, William Bouck Papers, Cornell University.
25 Holmes Hutchinson to William Bouck, June 14, 1831, William Bouck Papers, Cornell University.
26 Holmes Hutchinson to William Bouck, July 13, 1832, and August 16, 1832, William Bouck Papers, Cornell University.

obligation to the canal commissioners to build a quality product efficiently. The job had to be done correctly, which often meant that some changes had to be made, or work had to be redone. The contractor worked for himself. He sought to do the work as cheaply as possible to maximize his profit margin. Contractors were paid some money as certain stages of the work reached completion. The engineer, as the representative for the canal commissioners, inspected the work and determined how much had been completed by the contractor. If the engineer decided the job had not been done correctly, the contractor was not paid. If the contractor did not get paid, then neither did the subcontractor nor the workers. Such disputes often led to work being abandoned on canals by contractors, subcontractors, and workers.[27] The Chemung Canal was no exception.

Engineer Joseph Dana Allen believed some Chemung Canal contractors were fraudulent. Allen, who had complained about how slowly sections 16 and 17 were progressing, criticized the contractors who had asked for more money to complete the work. Allen reported to the canal commissioners, "I have paid them $50 on their work since you left, but really I fear the more they are paid, the worse the condition of the matter as relates to a dimmer resort. . . . I fear they will continue to expend more money upon the same amt. [sic] of work than might be done under more efficient and better management."[28] The contractors abandoned the contract in July 1832, and a new contractor took over the job.

One contract was abandoned when the contractor suddenly died. John Wynan of Big Flats contracted to build section 9 on the canal, but he died unexpectedly on August 29, 1831. The executors of his estate refused to complete the work he had contracted for. The contract had to be relet after the engineer declared Wynan's contract abandoned. The administrator of Wynan's estate later petitioned the New York State Canal Board to file a claim for money due to Wynan for the work he managed to complete. The estate received $310.[29]

While the contract system generated difficulties among the contractors, subcontractors, and engineers, it posed a more immediate threat to the workers. The workers, mainly recent Irish immigrants, labored under horrible conditions. Digging a canal was a difficult job and a hard life. Bad food, poor housing, alcohol abuse, and unsanitary conditions all contributed to the misery. Although few records survive about the workers on the Chemung Canal, accounts describing canal work on other contemporary canals help to shed light on what working on the Chemung Canal must have been like.

Typically the work day lasted from sunup to sundown. Breaks were allowed to eat meals, and short work stoppages were given to provide the men with whiskey. The men lived in hastily built shanties that were dirty and crowded. Often the shanties were not much better than the accommodations provided for the horses.

27 Way, *Common Labor*, pp. 59–68.

28 Joseph Dana Allen to William Bouck, May 20, 1832, William Bouck Papers, Cornell University; Annual Report of the Canal Commissioners, 1833, p.4.

29 *Annual Report of the Canal Commissioners*, 1832, p. 13; Petition to the Canal Board of New York State by Daniel Brown, administrator of the estate of John Wynan, Series A1140, February 24, 1834, New York State Archives.

The Chemung Canal could be a dangerous place. This newspaper article reported a murder during the construction of the canal. Murders, robberies, fights, and drownings were not uncommon events along the canal. (Elmira Gazette, Steele Memorial Library)

Pay could fluctuate anywhere from $14 to $26 per month, depending on the time of year and the demand for labor. The Lehigh Canal began construction in 1829, the same year the Chemung Canal gained approval. The Lehigh Canal offered wages of $14 per month with board included.[30]

Whiskey served as an added incentive for the workers. Employers made whiskey available during and after work. For the contractors, it provided a means to keep the workers complacent and working. For the worker, it provided an escape from the numbing work that seemed never-ending. It encouraged alcohol abuse that often led to greater misery and even death for the worker. A Rome, New York, resident who observed the workers on the Erie Canal commented: "It was a weird sight to see on a long line, both sides of the canal, hundreds of these wild Irishmen at work. Saturday nights in their board shanties, 'fighting drunk,' and contractors had to go in and club them right and left to quiet them. Whiskey and ague and fever did their legitimate work on great numbers."[31]

---

30 Way, *Common Labor*, pp. 142–3; Tobin, "Irish Labor on American Canals," p. 172.
31 Daniel Wager, ed., *Our County and Its People: A Descriptive Work on Oneida County, New York*, (Boston: The Boston History Company, 1892), p. 222.

People who observed construction on the Pennsylvania Canal in 1829 were appalled at the alcohol abuse being promoted. One witness commented: "There was plenty of whiskey on the works. . . . At night you could hear these wild Irish in their Bacchanalian revels fighting, singing, dancing, etc., all hours of the night."[32] The *Geneva Gazette and General Advertiser* reported:

> There have been repeated riots among the laborers on the Pennsylvania Canal, and two or three lives were recently lost by violence. It is said that *whiskey* was the cause of one of these fights, and if this *"drink of drunkards"* is as freely used there as it was in prose, cuting [sic] the internal improvements of this state, it is probable all of them may be attributed to the same cause. We have seen whiskey dealt out as freely as water, and while burning up the vitals of its unsuspecting victims, fatigue, languor and debility were the inevitable consequence.[33]

The Geneva newspaper editorialized for an end to supplying whiskey on the canals and encouraged contractors to increase wages and provide better food. Many citizens feared that public morals were being eroded by the attempt to improve the nation with public works.[34] Alcohol consumption in the United States had reached abominable levels by the 1830s. The per capita consumption of hard liquor reached over five gallons per year during that decade.[35]

It is highly probable that whiskey flowed abundantly at construction sites along the Chemung Canal. Canal workers expected it in addition to their wages. With so many canal projects in progress in both New York and Pennsylvania, the demand for labor would have made offering whiskey a near necessity in order to attract workers. Although alcohol abuse by the canal workers affronted the general public, it clearly had become a fixture within the work environment. One former contractor who worked on the Erie and Wabash Canal seemed to sum it up. When someone mentioned to him that the canal workers must have been drunk all of the time, the contractor replied, "You wouldn't expect them to work on the canal if they were sober would you?"[36]

Life along the canal stood in stark contrast to polite society. The hard life endured by canal workers bred desperate men. The Irish workers released pent-up anxieties about their dislocation from Ireland, alienation from society, and terrible working conditions by drinking and brawling. Murder and assaults were

---

32 Peter Way, "Evil Humors and Ardent Spirits: The Rough Culture of Canal Construction Laborers," *The Journal of American History* (March, 1993): 1413–4.

33 *Geneva Gazette and General Advertiser*, June 24, 1829, p. 3.

34 Ibid.

35 W. J. Rorabaugh, *The Alcoholic Republic* (New York: Oxford University Press, 1979), p. 8.

36 Peter Way, "Evil Humors and Ardent Spirits: The Rough Culture of Canal Construction Laborers," *The Journal of American History* (March, 1993): 1413–4.

---

not uncommon on the Chemung Canal. In April 1831 newspapers reported that the body of an Irish canal worker named Patrick DeLancey had been found in Big Flats near the feeder canal. He had been brutally beaten and stabbed. When last seen alive, DeLancey had over $1,000 in bank notes and certificates of deposit in his possession. Only $41 was found on his body. It was believed some money had been left with the dead man as part of an Irish superstition.[37]

Walking alone near the canal sometimes carried the risk of being assaulted and robbed. In the same month that Patrick DeLancey had been murdered, a man named Wilcox nearly met the same fate. Wilcox arrived in Havana (Montour Falls), left his things at the hotel there, and set out on foot along the canal towpath to visit an acquaintance who lived a short distance south of Havana. After Wilcox passed a shanty housing some canal laborers, he noticed that one man from the shanty had begun following him. Wilcox stopped to let the man pass, but the worker politely engaged in some conversation with Wilcox. The man directed Wilcox's attention to the lock pit filled with water they were standing near. When Wilcox turned to look, the man fiercely assaulted Wilcox, striking him with several blows to the head and face. The man had chosen the wrong person to assault. The strong and burly Wilcox seized his attacker in a mighty grip and shouted for help. The man was taken into custody. Barney Trainor, an Irish worker on the Chemung Canal, was tried and sentenced to jail.[38]

The bad food, poor sanitation, and close quarters generated another hazard among canal workers: disease. While many local people dreamed about the great economic bonanza the canal would make possible, they overlooked its ability to bring death to their doorstep. Greater commerce and contact with distant places also delivered contagions. The Irish migration supplied a needed work force to build the canals, but they also brought cholera to North America. In 1832, newspapers all across New York State tracked the deadly disease. It began in Quebec, where many Irish immigrants had arrived. The disease had been raging across Europe, and now it had arrived in North America. Towns along the Erie Canal were hit first, and many people along the Chemung Canal feared they were next.[39]

Holmes Hutchinson, the chief engineer on the Chemung Canal, worried about his family residing near Utica. Hutchinson wrote from Horseheads to Canal Commissioner William Bouck, expressing concern about cholera approaching Utica. He anxiously awaited letters from his family every day. He also feared the disease would soon strike the Chemung Canal. He wrote:

37 Rorabaugh, *The Alcoholic Republic*, 143–44; *Elmira Gazette*, April 16, 1831, p. 2; *Farmer's Advocate*, April 20, 1831, p. 3.

38 *Elmira Gazette*, April 30, 1831, excerpt from the *Havana Observer*, p. 2.

39 *Elmira Gazette*, June 30, 1832, p. 2; July 14, 1832, p. 3; July 21, 1832, p. 3; July 28, 1832, p. 2. All of these issues had reports of cholera from newspapers across the state.

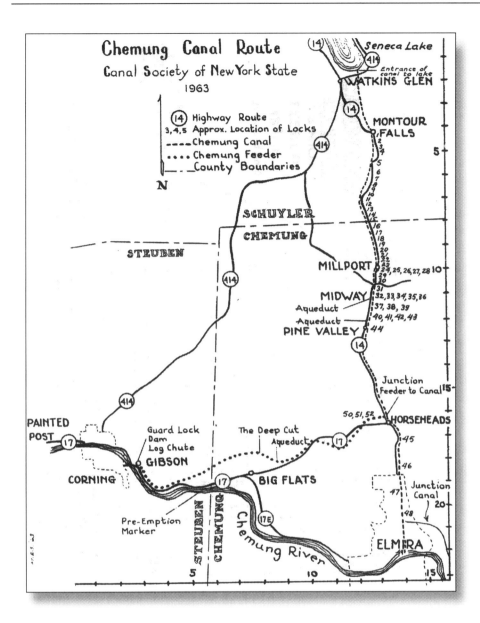

The main line of the Chemung Canal ran from the Chemung River in Elmira to Seneca Lake at Watkins Glen. Canal boats tied up at the harbor on Seneca Lake and were towed north to the Cayuga and Seneca Canal in Geneva. The feeder canal ran from the Chemung River at Gibson, near Corning, to Horseheads where it joined the main canal. The numbers shown alongside the canal route show the approximate location of the 53 locks on the Chemung Canal and Feeder. Note that most of the locks were found between Havana (Montour Falls) and Horseheads. Between those two points the land rose over 440 feet in elevation and required many locks. (Canal Society of New York State)

I am told there was two cases on a boat at Geneva on Sunday morning, one fatal—and there have been two cases in this vicinity within the last three days. The workmen on the line of the Canal are unusually healthy. [I] hope there never was a more quiet time of health than this season of the year than at the present period . . . .[40]

Diseases such as cholera and smallpox claimed the lives of some Chemung Canal workers. The dead were buried quickly to prevent spreading infection.[41] A few cases of cholera did strike the area near the canal, but the scare passed with little serious effect. Still, progress had brought a new threat that could strike at any moment. At various times during the canal's history, diseases such as cholera, smallpox, and scarlet fever made appearances that claimed lives and alarmed communities along the canal. A scarlet fever epidemic claimed many children in Millport in 1841, and in 1864 the town experienced an outbreak of smallpox. Smallpox also afflicted Big Flats in 1853.[42]

Despite the labor shortages, the shortcomings of the contract system, and the threat of cholera, the work moved forward. Optimists predicted the canal would be finished by September 1832, but poor construction and unforeseen difficulties worked to delay the opening further.

Given the nature of the huge task, it was inevitable that unforeseen problems arose. Some areas required extra excavation. Some lock locations had to be moved due to quicksand or flood damages, and the canal route itself had to be moved in some instances. Even after the canal had been completed and opened, many contractors and subcontractors continued seeking extra allowances for work they performed on the Chemung Canal. The various extra expenses had caused many to lose money, and they petitioned the state canal board to compensate them beyond the contract price. In most cases, the board obliged them.[43]

Human error also delayed the canal. Once the canal prism had been excavated to its proper depth and width, the bottom and sides had to be "puddled." A suitable material, usually clay, had to be placed in the prism so that it would hold water. On sections 2 and 3, the puddling had been done improperly. Upon letting

40 Holmes Hutchinson to William Bouck, August 16, 1832, William Bouck Papers, Cornell University.
41 Frank Severne, "The Chemung Canal and its Construction," *Watkins Express*, August 10, 1955, folder on Canals, Schuyler County Historical Society.
42 Towner, *A History of the Valley and County of Chemung*, 548; *Havana Journal*, May 21, 1853, p. 2, The *Havana Journal* reported a case about a canal boathand taken ill upon returning from New York City. It was believed he had smallpox. Soon afterwards, five others, including members of the boatman's family and the boat captain's family, also fell ill; *Havana Journal*, August 20, 1853, p. 2; April, 23, 1864, p. 2.
43 Petition of Luke Hitchcock and Company to the Canal Board of New York State, April 1833; Petition of Westlake and McConnell to the Canal Board of New York State, March 5, 1834; Petition of Caleb Hammel to the Canal Board of New York State, March 12, 1834; Petition of Phineas Tuttle to the Canal Board of New York State, March 11, 1834. All the mentioned petitions were from Series A1140, Packets 26 and 27, New York State Archives.

This photograph, taken around 1870, shows the bridge over the Chemung River at Gibson. In the right foreground the guard lock can be seen. In the right background the dam on the river is visible. (Chemung County Historical Society)

the water in to test it in 1832, the gravelly soil beneath the clay washed away, causing the canal to leak badly. The water had to be drained and the work redone.[44]

By July 1832, the canal appeared to be nearly finished. A Fourth of July celebration in Horseheads signaled the community's expectations that the canal would soon be open. After some orations, the festivities included a ride on the Chemung Canal:

> The forward boat contained the Field Piece, Martial Music, and citizens; the second the ladies, Band of Music, and Committees of Arrangements; the third Citizens in general. After the ride, being six miles coming and returning, the company retired highly gratified. Good feeling and harmony prevailed through-out the day.[45]

The *Elmira Gazette* proudly announced that the canal would open by the end of September. Some merchants eagerly anticipated the chance to ship merchandise on the new canal, and they began stockpiling goods in Horseheads to

44 *Annual Report of the Canal Commissioners,* 1833, p. 26.
45 *Elmira Gazette,* July 14, 1832, p. 1.

A seven-foot-high dam across the Chemung River created a pool of water that supplied most of the water for the Chemung Canal. Other smaller sources of water had to be utilized along the canal during the summer months when water levels were low. The dam was located at Gibson at a spot called the Chimney Narrows, named for the rock formation found along the river. The dam included a chute so that timber rafts could pass by it, but many rafters disliked the dam and the chute. Notice in the photograph that some people in a small boat are about to pass over the dam. *(History of Corning–Painted Post)*

await the opening. To their disappointment the canal did not open, and many goods were lost.[46]

While the canal appeared to be finished, another setback prevented it from opening for business. The decision to use wooden rather than stone locks proved to be shortsighted. When the water was let in to test the locks, many leaked badly. The water pressure caused the sides to bow. At great expense, the locks had to be

46 *Annual Report of the Canal Commissioners, 1833*, p. 27.

equipped with better support. After experimenting with the worst locks, engineers Holmes Hutchinson and Joseph Dana Allen discovered that by bolting the longitudinal sill more securely to the bottom sill with 22 T-shaped iron bolts and by bracing the walls better on each side, the locks would work. The extra work required expending an additional $8,000.[47] From the very beginning the wooden locks were inadequate, and they continued to be a nuisance throughout the canal's history.

All the mistakes and delays meant more expense, and the Chemung Canal went over budget. It had been projected to cost a little over $280,000 to build, but it ultimately required spending $314,395.51. Since the Chemung Canal law had allotted only $300,000 to construct the canal, a bill had to be introduced to appropriate an extra $16,000. The appropriation received approval in spring 1832. Despite the extra expense, the Chemung Canal still cost less to build per mile than any other state canal.[48]

After working on the defective locks all winter, the canal finally reached completion in 1833. A celebration in Elmira in May marked the canal opening. A boat normally used to carry stone for building purposes on the Chemung River was commandeered for the event. Passengers were charged a shilling to ride from Elmira to Pine Valley. The crowded boat meant standing room only for many passengers. With flags flying the boat navigated the canal as speeches were made and songs were sung.[49]

Geneva rejoiced just as much as Elmira to finally have the canal opened. On May 15 a Geneva newspaper reported: "We are highly gratified to announce that the Chemung Canal is completed and navigable from Elmira to Havana at the head of this Lake. A Boat has passed the whole distance."[50] The following week 30 fully loaded boats left Geneva, headed for the Chemung Canal. Those on board had no idea that another disaster had already struck.

On May 5 heavy rain began to fall, and it continued for the next two days. The rain fell particularly hard on the evening of May 7. The Chemung River and the many nearby streams swelled to overflowing and a terrible flood ravaged the canal. In Horseheads, Sing Sing Creek cut through the banks of the feeder canal and carried a great deal of gravel into the canal bed. The aqueduct that carried the canal over Sing Sing Creek also sustained some damage.

The worst destruction happened along Catharine Creek. The fall in elevation from Horseheads to Seneca Lake helped to make the waters in Catharine Creek especially destructive. The rushing water breached the canal embankment and washed away embankments and towpaths. The flood waters carried away most of the wooden docking that had been intended to help protect the canal.

---

47 Ibid., pp. 26–27; Joseph Dana Allen to William Bouck, November 4, 1832, and Holmes Hutchinson to William Bouck, September 21, 1832, William Bouck Papers, Cornell University.

48 William Bouck to Comptroller Silas Wright, May 30, 1832, William Bouck Papers, Cornell University; *Ithaca Journal*, excerpt from the *Assembly Journal*, March 28, 1832, p. 2; Whitford, *History of the Canal System*, pp. 616–17.

49 Towner, *A History of the Valley and County of Chemung*, pp. 125–6.

50 *Geneva Gazette and Mercantile Advertiser*, May 15, 1833, p. 3; May 22, 1833, p. 3.

This photograph shows Hanover Square in Horseheads looking north around 1870. The white building in the background just beyond the intersection was the toll collector's office for the Chemung Canal. The office was located at the juncture of the feeder canal and the Chemung Canal. Boats had to pay the toll on their cargo at this office. There was another toll collector in Havana (Montour Falls) to collect tolls on boats headed south from Seneca Lake and on those that began their journey north of the Horseheads office. The first toll collector in the Horseheads office was Thomas Maxwell, who had worked diligently to get the canal bill passed. Today, the site of the Horseheads collection office is the Horseheads Fire Department. The canal prism can still be seen there. (Chemung County Historical Society)

Many locks received only slight damage although some supports for the sides were damaged or carried off.

Fortunately, the newly reinforced locks suffered minimal damage. The canal from Elmira to Horseheads suffered almost no damage, but private property owners were not so lucky. Many mills along Catharine Creek were ravaged when their mill dams were destroyed by the raging waters, and some buildings were washed away. [51]

Before the storm had arrived, the area had been experiencing a drought. Many timber rafts lined the river banks, awaiting the high water that spring always delivered. The drought left them stranded. Some rafts got stuck on sandbars in the Chemung River and its tributaries. The May rainfall came to their rescue, but the rescue quickly turned into a disaster. The downpour swelled the streams quickly and sent rafts and large logs careening down the river.

The feeder dam on the Chemung River at Gibson received only slight damage. The fast moving river water had undercut some abutments, causing the dam to settle in places. Once the flood waters subsided many raftsmen attempted to utilize the high water to get their goods to market, but the feeder dam impeded

51 *Annual Report of the Canal Commissioners*, 1834, pp. 17–20; *Ithaca Journal*, May 29, 1833, excerpt from the *Elmira Republican*, pp. 2–3; *Geneva Gazette and Mercantile Advertiser*, June 5, 1833, excerpt from the *Elmira Gazette*, p. 3.

their journey to the Susquehanna River. Although the dam was equipped with a chute to allow passage for rafts and canoes, it often made their passage more dangerous. The sudden drop down the incline into deep water frequently caused the rafts to break apart.

Some raftsmen decided to remedy the problem. They began to dismantle the dam and to set fire to it. Summoned to the scene, the superintendent of the Chemung Canal, Wyatt Carr, got into an argument with the raftsmen, who threatened to throw him into the river. Carr finally got the men to calm down and helped them get their raft through. He remained at the dam the next day to assist other raftsmen. Thanks to Carr, the vandalism to the dam was kept at a minimum.[52]

Although the canal had sustained some serious damage, inspections showed that it had fared better overall than previously thought. Canal Commissioners William Bouck and William Hoffman happened to be in Elmira to inspect the new canal when the flood struck, and they immediately launched preparations to begin repairs. Estimates predicted that repairs would cost from $11,000 to $15,000. Many men quickly went to work fixing embankments, replacing towpaths, and shoring up the locks and dam.[53]

Early reports expressed confidence that the Chemung Canal would be operable by July 1, but that proved overly optimistic. In late August boats began navigating the canal again, yet sections still remained closed. The southern portion from Horseheads to Elmira still had not opened, and neither had the feeder. The entire canal did not open for business until November.[54]

An early Corning resident recalled the first boat to arrive in Corning from the Chemung Canal. A group of men met the boat below the feeder dam to convince the captain to enter the Chemung River and unload his cargo at the Corning warehouse. The captain feared losing his boat and cargo over the dam, but after much persuasion, he finally capitulated and safely made the journey on the river to a warehouse just below the dam.[55] This inaugurated the canal trade that would make Corning a thriving port.

The Chemung Canal had opened for business. The toll collectors, Thomas Maxwell at Horseheads and Frederick Ritter at Havana, began carrying out their duties as boats finally navigated the canal. The first season ended quickly since the canal had to close for the winter in mid-December. The tolls collected amounted to only $694, but great hopes for the future persisted.[56] The canal had been created to improve commerce, and now the communities stood poised to enter a new age.

52 *Ithaca Journal*, May 29, 1833, excerpt from the *Elmira Republican*, pp.2–3; *Annual Report of the Canal Commissioners*, 1834, pp. 19–20.
53 *Ithaca Journal*, May 29, 1833, excerpt from the *Elmira Republican*, p. 2; *Geneva Gazette and Mercantile Advertiser*, June 5, 1833, excerpt from the *Elmira Gazette*, p. 3.
54 *Geneva Gazette and Mercantile Advertiser*, August 21, 1833, p. 3; November 13, 1833, p. 3.
55 *Corning Journal*, July 2, 1857, p. 2.
56 Whitford, *History of the Canal System*, 1064; "Canal Appointments by the Canal Board," *Ithaca Journal*, April 10, 1833, p. 2; *Annual Report of the Canal Commissioners*, 1834, p. 20.

This wintertime photograph shows the Chemung Canal looking west on Second Street. Note the canal boat next to the T. Briggs and Company Steam Brewery. The bridge on Second Street carried the road over the canal. The canal closed in the winter, usually by the first week in December, and re-opened again in late April or early May. The frozen canal made ice skating a popular recreation during the cold months. (Chemung County Historical Society)

CHAPTER THREE

The Great Emporium

THE PRESENCE OF THE CHEMUNG CANAL ushered in a new era for the towns along its banks. It brought an economic boom that led to land speculation, new business, a cash economy, and population growth. It became a business unto itself, spawning many ancillary services catering to the boatmen and workers. Groceries, boatyards, hotels, and taverns dotted the landscape along the canal. For many people, the canal meant an opportunity to profit, but it also created greater opportunity for consumption. Goods became available in wide varieties. Many items that had been difficult or impossible to acquire began to pour into the area from New York City, Europe, and the Caribbean.

It appeared the canal offered boundless progress for the local area, but people quickly learned that progress also had its price. The canal culture that arose included a wage-earning work force composed mainly of Irish immigrants who indulged in fighting, excessive drinking, and foul language. The workers' intemperance led to violence, crime, and strikes, which in turn provoked disdain and fear among the local citizens. Dependent on their wages and their employers, many canal workers labored on the Sabbath rather than attend church. The upper class viewed the canal workers as a threat to their society and took steps to exert control over them, including manipulating them at election time.

The canal also had negative effects on the landscape. Once the canal opened the door to distant markets, local timber became a valuable commodity. Lumbermen stripped the landscape bare to fill the growing demand. Lumbering became a major industry and supplied much business to the canal, but the practices the industry relied upon destroyed itself and damaged the land. The vanishing forest meant more flooding during heavy rainfalls and less water during dry spells. The many floods damaged the canal and required costly repairs. Dry summer months reduced the available water needed to keep the canal operating.

Landowners whose property lay in the path of progress discovered another negative impact when they found access to their land cut off by the canal. Without a bridge to cross the canal, they could not use some of their land. Catharine Fridley of Big Flats petitioned the canal commissioners for damages because the feeder canal divided her property, cutting her off from five acres of her land and a spring that was her main source of water. Without a bridge over the canal, she lost the use of that part of her property and asked for damages in the amount of $270. The canal appraisers refused her claim in 1837 on the grounds that it was not made out or signed in her own handwriting.[1]

Vincent Conkling of Horseheads found himself in a similar situation. Conkling, who had lobbied to get the canal built and had even contributed to building a section of it, complained to Canal Commissioner William Bouck that without a bridge over the canal he was cut off from some of his land. George Coryell, who owned a sawmill, also complained to William Bouck because the canal denied him access to some of his wooded land. He was left with timber he could not cut and with little space to stack the boards he had.[2]

At first, people envisioned only the positive effects the canal would bring. The Chemung Canal opened the door to many opportunities for the people it served, and many scrambled to capitalize upon it. Land speculation was one of the first ways in which people profited from the canal. Land adjoining the canal became valuable even before the first dirt had been turned. In Elmira, a land battle took place over where to locate the canal through the town. The Baldwin and Maxwell families competed with the Tuttle and Covell families over whose land would provide the path for the canal. The Tuttle and Covell faction wanted the canal to run through the more settled area where their families owned land, while the Baldwin and Maxwell faction endorsed a location on their land in the westerly and less populated side of town. The Baldwins and Maxwells won out and profited as their land value increased. They quickly began selling lots along the canal.

In July 1830 the *Elmira Gazette* carried several advertisements offering land for sale near the canal. One offered a house and lot on Baldwin and Water Streets with this sales pitch:

> It is near the termination of the Chemung Canal—a most important situation for a public house, or business of any kind . . . . By the aid of this [canal] a rapid and extensive growth of the village must be the consequence, and no place in our western country can hold out more solid inducements to the Capitalist or industrious Mechanic to make speedy investments. —*Isaac Baldwin.*

1 Assembly Documents, no. 99, "Report of the Canal Commissioners on the Petition of Catharine Fridley," February 1, 1837.
2 Howard Conkling to William Bouck, August 14, 1834, and George Coryell to William Bouck, September 22, 1833, William Bouck Papers, Cornell University.

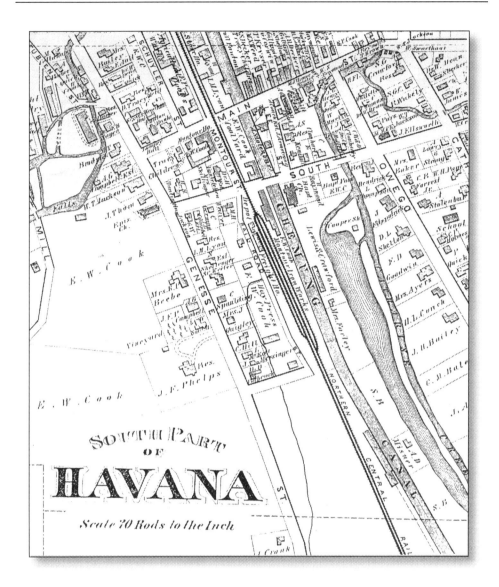

The map shows the village of Havana (present-day Montour Falls) in 1874. Activity in Havana centered around the Chemung Canal. Many businesses located along the canal: flouring mill, sawmill, coal yard, iron works, and a pottery business. After the canal closed, the prism was filled in for health reasons. Canal Street in Montour Falls was once the Chemung Canal. The canal crossed Main Street where the village post office and the Montour Pharmacy are located today. (*Atlas of Schuyler County, New York.* Philadelphia: Pomeroy, Whitman and Company, 1874. Montour Falls Memorial Library)

The same newspaper carried an advertisement for "30 lots, on the west side of Canal Street, being 40 feet on the Canal Street, and extending back to the canal." Another offer promoted lots "situated on Water Street between the bridge and the southerly termination of the Chemung Canal, and are probably the most commanding business locations in the village. —For terms or other information apply to Baldwin and Maxwell."[3]

As the digging progressed near Horseheads, advertisements offering land for sale near that village began to appear. One ad touted a farm located three miles from Elmira and two miles from Horseheads as a good investment because the canal would pass right through it. A mill had been located there, but a fire had destroyed the structure. The race and dam were not harmed by the fire, leaving open the possibility for an enterprising person to restore the mill. Another advertisement for a farm described it as "only 1/4 mile from the Chemung Canal and 2 miles north of Dundee [Horseheads]."[4]

Holmes Hutchinson, the engineer who oversaw the Chemung Canal construction, demonstrated his confidence in the canal by joining in the land speculation. Hutchinson bought land in Horseheads in 1830, surveyed it, and marked it into lots that eventually became incorporated into the village. In 1837, the residents incorporated the village as Fairport but changed the name back to Horseheads in 1845.[5]

The opportunities presented by the Chemung Canal made locating near it important for entrepreneurs. Taverns, hotels, mills, groceries, and many other businesses sprang up near the canal. Isaac Baldwin created a basin near the terminus of the canal in Elmira to provide a place where boats could dock to load or unload cargoes before beginning their return trip. Boatmen could conveniently visit nearby taverns and hotels that sprang into business with the creation of the canal. During the canal construction, the Elmira Hotel opened for business at the northwest corner of what is now State and East Water Streets, and the Mansion House began serving spirits and meals at the corner of Lake and Market Streets. Nearby stood the Black Horse Tavern at Lake and Water Streets, whose existence preceded the canal. The Eagle Tavern opened on Water Street in 1833. Hogan's Tavern, near Baldwin Street, served as a bailiwick for the Irishmen who dug the Chemung Canal.[6]

The Elmira Rolling Mills, which made iron strap rails for the railroads, opened beside the Chemung Canal in Elmira in 1859. Both the railroad and the canal had access to the mills to bring them iron ore and to haul the finished product. At its peak, the company employed over 400 mainly Irish and Welsh workers.

3   *Elmira Gazette*, July 17, 1830, p. 3.
4   *Elmira Gazette*, January 15, 1831, p. 1; March 19, 1831, p. 3; The *Elmira Gazette* carried a notice on page 2 of the November 6, 1830 issue that the citizens of Horseheads voted at a public meeting to change the name of their village to Dundee. That name proved to be short lived.
5   Towner, *A History of the Valley and County of Chemung*, p. 473.
6   Ibid., 125, 134–6; Mary Clare Lineham, "A History of the Irish in America," *Elmira College Bulletin*, Chapter 3, (August, 1925): p. 3.

Other businesses that located along the canal in Elmira included a flour mill, a feed mill, a warehouse, a foundry, and a coal yard.[7]

In Havana, Charles Cook built the Montour House just a few yards from the canal. When it opened for business in 1854, it served as a hotel, tavern, and office building. He also built a flouring mill and a sawmill alongside the canal shortly after the canal opened and opened the Montour Iron Works near the canal in 1850. Cook added a coal yard, planing mill, and carriage shop all adjoining the canal. A brickyard, pottery works, woolen mill, and boatyards operated by the canal in Havana as well. Life in Havana clearly centered around the canal.[8]

At Gibson, where the feeder canal began near Corning, a gristmill, sawmill, carding mill, dye house, and tavern served the public. John Gibson also erected a large planing mill. A boatyard to build canal boats also opened along the canal at Gibson.[9]

Boat building became a popular industry at various sites along the Chemung Canal. The area abounded with timber to supply the new industry with raw materials, and the Chemung Canal and other state canals kept up a steady demand for canal boats. Elmira, Millport, Corning, and Havana each built boats for use on canals throughout New York State. The *Corning Journal* told its readers in 1849: "A new and beautiful Canal Boat has just made her appearance at our docks bearing the name Charles C. B. Walker. She was built in the boatyard of Mr. King, in this town, under the direction and superintendence of Mr. Miner, an experienced Boat Builder from Seneca Falls."[10]

In Havana, canal boat building became an active enterprise. Launching a new canal boat became a social event. Nearly 150 people gathered in Havana to watch a new craft get launched in the W. C. Gillespie boatyard in May 1862. A Buffalo man bought the boat, and he in turn sold it to another man in New York City for $3,000. The boat launching marked the second for that season by the Gillespie boatyard, which was busy working on a third boat.[11]

Elmira also had boatyards. One operated on the river bank near the Lake Street bridge, and another constructed boats along the banks of the canal; however, neither Elmira nor Havana could claim to be the chief boat-building center for the canal. That title belonged to Millport.

At its peak, Millport had six boatyards making a variety of canal vessels. The boats that were manufactured included "lakers," which had a curved bow like an ocean-going vessel, and "scows," which had a straight bow. Local lumber supplied pine or hemlock planks 70 feet long, 3 inches thick, and 14 to 16 inches

7 S. Edward Rose, "Rolling Mills Flourished 30 Years," *Elmira Sunday Telegram*, July 18, 1948, Folder 265–225, "Rolling MIlls," Chemung County Historical Society; *Elmira Gazette*, November 25, 1918, Chemung County Historical Society, Folder 0640, "Canals."
8 Wayne Morrison Sr., ed., *Early History, & c., Havana, New York*, (Ovid, New York: W. C. Morrison & Co., printers, no date), pp. 120, 225–26, 65.
9 Dimitroff and Janes, *History of the Corning-Painted Post Area*, pp. 29–30.
10 *Corning Journal*, May 16, 1849, p. 2.
11 *Havana Journal*, May 3, 1862, p. 2.

wide to build the canal boats. Chemung Canal boats often were 60 feet long and as much as 15 feet wide. At the bow a stabling area provided for the horses or mules, and in the stern a galley furnished a crude dining area and bunks. With all the stores, mills, and boatyards located at Millport by the 1840s, it appeared to many that Millport would become more prosperous and larger than Elmira.[12] Unfortunately for Millport, the entire economy centered around the canal, and when the canal closed, the town witnessed a decline.

The grocery business, like boatyards, offered another opportunity for people to profit from the canal. Many groceries sprang into existence adjacent to the canal and catered to boatmen and canal workers. Boatmen and their families lived on the canal boats during the shipping season, and they needed to buy supplies as they traveled. The many locks from Havana to Horseheads allowed the boats to navigate the rise in landscape. Of the 53 locks on the entire canal, 44 of them were located from Havana to Horseheads. It took a long time to move through the locks that followed one another in rapid succession. As their boats slowly navigated the myriad of locks near Millport, boatmen left their boats and crews to visit a nearby grocery store. While they purchased flour, sugar, and other basic items, they also often purchased whiskey. A grocery frequently doubled as a saloon.

Since so many groceries owed their existence to the canal, they welcomed the boatmen. Grocery store advertisements often pictured a canal boat since many stores were located close to the canal. An ad in the *Havana Journal* in 1858 spoke directly to canal workers about the store's proprietor: "BOATMEN will please bear in mind that he has every article of dress they may desire, and will furnish quite as liberally as the largest city establishments." Another advertisement said, "To say to Boatmen, Raftsmen, and the community at large, that TAYLOR & ROWLEY are prepared and anxious to serve them, would be to tell them what they already know."[13]

Location on the canal inspired many people to open stores. In 1829, the year the Chemung Canal was authorized, Havana had only four grocery stores. By 1853, a newspaper from another canal town commented, "Havana has a population of about 1,300 and nine dry goods merchants advertise in their village paper; Lyons has a population of more than 3,000 and not one dry goods merchant."[14] As early as 1836, Elmira could already boast 19 general stores; Horseheads had six.[15]

The many stores the canal made possible offered goods previously not available in the local area and inaugurated an increased demand for consumer commodities. The canal gave local communities contact with the Great Lakes and

12 Towner, *History of the Valley and County of Chemung*, 127; "2 Deaths Recall Millport History of Canal Period," undated newspaper article folder CF 0640, Chemung County Historical Society; *Elmira Sunday Telegram*, December 23, 1923; W. Charles Barber, "The Chemung Canal: It Drew Wealth (and Rascals) to Elmira," *Elmira Sunday Telegram*, August 9, 1953, "canals" folder, Chemung County Historical Society.

13 *Havana Journal*, December 8, 1849, p. 4; August 21, 1858, p. 2; May 23, 1857, p. 2.

14 *Geneva Gazette and General Advertiser*, April 29, 1829, p. 3; *Havana Journal*, May 7, 1853, excerpt from the Lyons newspaper, p. 3.

15 Thomas Gordon, *Gazetteer of the State of New York* (Philadelphia: Collins Printers, 1836), pp. 725–26.

There were many locks on the Chemung Canal near Millport. The numerous locks slowed traffic on the canal, and often boatmen left their canal boat to visit a grocery to buy needed supplies, have a drink, or visit friends. They later caught up on foot with the canal boat farther down the line. Millport was a busy town with many mills, boat-building shops, and groceries. (The Booth Library of the Chemung County Historical Society)

New York City. New York harbors served as gateways to Europe and the Caribbean. In 1835 George G. Pattison's dry goods and grocery store advertised that it had Cuban and Puerto Rican molasses for sale. By 1836 the Haight and Holmes grocery store in Elmira invited customers to visit its store to buy Jamaican and St. Croix rum, Holland gin, mackerel and codfish, as well as molasses from New Orleans. Also in Elmira, Luce and Perry Grocers had fresh oysters, cocoa, figs, raisins, coffee, codfish, cloves, cinnamon, and mackerel. In Havana, S. C. Ayers advertised in 1839 that his store had oranges and lemons for sale and that his wife had a variety of fashionable millinery from New York for the ladies to buy. A Millport grocer had India rubber overshoes, Brazil nuts, almonds, codfish, and mackerel for sale.[16]

The increased trade generated by the canal also contributed a change in the local economy from subsistence and barter to a market economy. Before the Chemung Canal opened, many business transactions involved barter. Local store advertisements before 1833 often informed consumers that goods could be purchased for cash or produce. McReynolds' Dry Goods and Groceries in Elmira

16 *Elmira Weekly Gazette*, July 25, 1835, p. 3; August 6, 1836, p. 3; *Elmira Gazette*, December 23, 1837, p. 3; *Havana Republican*, January 30, 1839, p. 3; May 10, 1837, p. 3; December 5, 1838, p. 3.

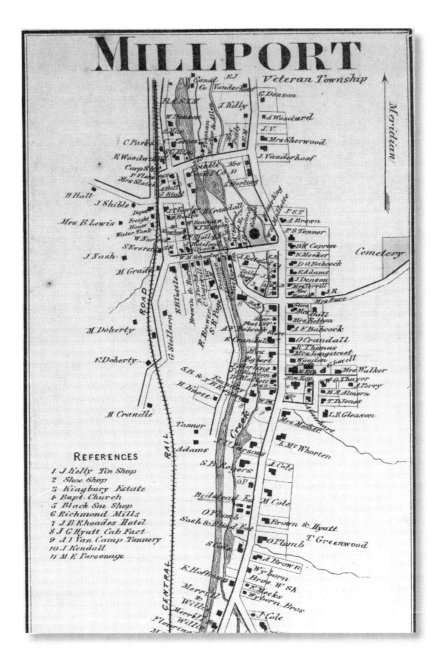

MILLPORT

Veteran Township

REFERENCES
1 J Kelly Tin Shop
2 Shoe Shop
3 Kingbury Estate
4 Bapt. Church
5 Black Sm Shop
6 Richmond Mills
7 J B Rhoades Hotel
8 J G Hyatt Cab Fact
9 A I Van Camp Tannery
10 J Kendall
11 M E Parsonage

With the passage of the Chemung Canal in 1829, Millvale changed its name to Millport. Millport prospered due to the canal. Many sawmills took advantage of the water from the canal and the creek to turn the surrounding forests into lumber. Lumber made up one of the greatest commodities shipped on the canal. Catharine Creek ran parallel to the Chemung Canal through Millport and along much of the way to Montour Falls. Nearly every year the creek flooded and caused havoc with the canal. (Author's personal collection)

advertised that its merchandise could be purchased "at the lowest prices, for Cash or most kinds of merchantable produce." Beckwith and Satterly's grocery informed buyers that it had the "lowest retail prices for Cash or Country Produce." Cabinetmakers Vail and Stephenson would take lumber, produce, and cash as payment for their work.[17]

The market exchange made possible by the Chemung Canal brought greater demands for cash. Once the canal opened, few businesses showed a willingness to accept barter or credit. They wanted cash. As one contemporary observer noted: "[T]he opening of the canal required other changes in the way of doing business. A circulating medium became absolutely necessary, the wider and more complicated interests demanding some other system than that long in vogue, barter."[18] Hall's Dry Goods and Groceries and J. B. Post and Sons' Grocery, both in Elmira, were among the many businesses that invited buyers to patronize their stores in 1838 with cash only. In 1839 grocery store owner F. F. Fairman announced that his new store was "on the entire cash system."[19]

The trade created by the Chemung Canal linked the area to a market economy requiring cash and credit. Local banks received charters to meet the cash needs demanded by the growing economy. Before the canal opened, the closest banks were in Ithaca and Geneva, which made getting credit difficult. In 1833 the legislature passed a bill chartering the Chemung Canal Bank in Elmira.[20] The Bank of Corning capitalized in 1839. In 1851 the Bank of Havana received a charter from the state largely due to efforts by Charles Cook.[21] Local banks made available the cash and credit that sustained economic growth. Banking also financed local enterprises such as lumbering, coal mining, and railroads, which created even more jobs and wealth.

Lumber and coal had been two important reasons for building the Chemung Canal. Shipping those two commodities quickly became the canal's chief business. The heavily timbered land surrounding the canal contained abundant white pine, spruce, oak, elm, hemlock, and maple.[22] Although local sawmills existed before the canal, the canal provided a ready market for lumber. Sawmills sprang up, and lumbermen bared the landscape to meet the insatiable demand for lumber and firewood. The timber became homes and plank roads, as well as railroad ties and fuel to burn in railroad engines.

17 *Elmira Gazette*, October 9, 1830, pp. 3–4; January 22, 1831, p. 1.
18 Towner, *History of the Valley and County of Chemung*, p. 146.
19 *Elmira Gazette*, September 29, 1838, p. 2; October 19, 1839, p. 3.
20 *Elmira Gazette*, February 12, 1831, p. 3; September 29, 1838, p. 2; Towner, *A History of the Valley and County of Chemung*, pp. 146–47. Today, the Chemung Valley History Museum and Chemung County Historical Society are located in the original Chemung Canal Bank building.
21 Dimitroff and Janes, *History of the Corning-Painted Post Area*, p. 30; Morrison, ed., *Early History &c., Havana, New York*, p. 123.
22 Morrison, *Early History &c., Havana, New York*, p. 723.

The lumber business boomed along the canal for over 20 years. In Elmira, pine boards and shingles stood stacked along the canal from Market Street to Second Street, awaiting transport to Albany and other cities along the Erie Canal.[23] Immediately after the canal opened, lumbering became the main industry in Big Flats. By 1852 one-sixth of the lumber received in Albany came from Corning. The Erie Railroad had been bringing large amounts of lumber to Corning from the western New York counties for shipment on the Chemung Canal. In 1851 over 35 million feet of lumber cleared the port at Corning. By 1852 the amount had surpassed 51 million feet, and the following year it topped 87 million feet.[24]

The numerous creeks near the canal provided accessible water power for many mills. Newtown, Sing Sing, and Catharine Creeks supplied the water power for sawmills and gristmills. Many mills were located near the canal to utilize the water power and easy shipping. Millvale, a village located between the summit level and Havana, offered the best example. In 1829, upon learning that the legislature had approved construction of the Chemung Canal, the town changed its name to Millport. At its peak, Millport supported 17 mills, most of which were sawmills. The ample mills provided employment, and the numerous locks near Millport slowed canal traffic to a crawl, allowing crews to leave their boats to shop. Millport became the busiest place along the canal.[25]

Records from the toll collector's office at Havana reflect the bustling lumber activity near Millport. Any goods that came from Corning or Elmira would have paid their tolls at the Horseheads collectors' office, so tolls paid on lumber at Havana would have come from the area between Horseheads and Havana. The Havana toll collector's reports for 1854 and 1855 list lumber shipments as the largest contributor to the toll collections. In 1854, the Havana toll collector took in $15,154, over 70 percent from tolls on lumber products. Lumber tolls accounted for over $8,000 of the $14,485 in toll receipts in 1855.[26]

A reported disaster on Seneca Lake helps to show how important the lumber trade became. Steamships towed canal boats and rafts north on Seneca Lake from Watkins Glen to Geneva. The steamship *Ben Loder* was headed to Geneva with 27 canal boats and 17 cribs filled with timber in tow when a sudden storm with high winds began to toss the boats and rafts. Eleven boats broke away from the towline. They were recovered after the storm, but one had capsized, and several had filled with water. The newspaper account reported that lumber made up the greatest commodity aboard the boats and rafts. Six of the 11 boats that broke away were filled with lumber. Added to the 17 cribs also filled with timber, it would appear that even by 1861 lumber still maintained its place as an important commodity being shipped on the Chemung Canal.[27]

23 Towner, *History of the Valley and County of Chemung*, pp. 163–64.
24 Ibid., 502; *Havana Journal*, April 23, 1853, p. 2; *Corning Journal*, January 15, 1851, p. 2; "Port of Corning," *Corning Journal*, April 29, 1853, p. 2; *Annual Report of the Canal Commissioners*, 1854, p. 84.
25 Towner, *History of the Valley and County of Chemung*, p. 547; Barber, "The Chemung Canal," 6c.
26 *Trade and Tonnage Annual Report for Havana, New York, 1854 and 1855*, Montour Falls Memorial Library.
27 *Havana Journal*, May 25, 1861, p. 2.

Unfortunately for the lumber industry at the time, little was done about conservation or reforestation. Clear-cutting reigned as the preferred method. Wasteful forest management ultimately destroyed the industry in the area, and lumber businesses and people moved on to more heavily forested locales farther west. By the mid-1870s, the larger lumber businesses near the Chemung Canal found the local timber supply inadequate to maintain their livelihood. Many folded or moved west.[28]

The assault on the forests by the lumber companies had a tremendous effect on the environment that proved detrimental to the canal. The treeless landscape and the greater cultivation resulting from the increase in farms led to more runoff. The end result meant less water in the summer months for the canal as the Chemung River level declined. It also meant, paradoxically, more disastrous floods after heavy rains.[29] Deforestation in the Upper Delaware River Valley had similar results. Like the Chemung Canal, the trees along the streams in the Upper Delaware drainage were removed first. It led to powerful floods through the 1850s and 1860s that caused tremendous property damage and loss of life.[30] The environmental impact of the Chemung Canal ultimately contributed to the canal's own demise as flooding and insufficient water increased operating costs.

When the lumber industry began its decline in the area, demand for another commodity rose. Dwindling forests led the nation to turn increasingly to coal as a fuel. The demand for coal grew larger with each decade, and the volume that needed to be transported grew also. Use of the Chemung Canal provided a temporary solution. Although the railroads could more speedily meet the demand, for a time the canals could transport coal more cheaply. The Chemung Canal became an important link between the Pennsylvania coal fields and the Erie Canal. Ironically, coal had been an important reason for building the Chemung Canal, and coal would have a hand in closing the canal as demand outstripped the canal's ability to meet it.

Elmira, only 20 miles from Athens, Pennsylvania, on the north branch of the Susquehanna River, appeared to have a good location for accessing the coal trade. Even before the Chemung Canal opened, many people recognized how important it would be to connect Elmira and Athens by water. A water route between the two communities would provide an easy passage for coal barges. Some Elmira businessmen met in December 1837 to draft resolutions to the New York State legislature, seeking to extend the Chemung Canal to the state line and eventually to connect it with the Pennsylvania canal system. Nearly 20 years would pass before their vision became reality. In 1855 the Junction Canal, a private enterprise, opened for business. Its president, John Arnot from Elmira,

28 Dimitroff and Janes, *History of the Corning-Painted Post Area*, p. 77.
29 Canal Commissioner Henry Fitzhugh to O. C. Hartwell, Division Engineer, November 11, 1856, excerpt from the *Annual Report of the Canal Commissioners*, 1857, p. 84.
30 Robert McGregor, "Radical Environmental Change: Deforestation in the Upper Delaware River Valley, 1800–1875," (Ph.D diss., Binghamton University, 1984), pp.183–84.

Havana (Montour Falls) during the Civil War. In the foreground is the bridge over the canal on Main Street. In the left background is the Montour House built by Charles Cook. The three men across the bridge and to the left are said to be reading about the war in the newspaper. (Montour Falls Memorial Library)

had been an early advocate for the Junction Canal. The Junction Canal connected the Chemung Canal in Elmira to the Chemung River at Wilawana, Pennsylvania. The following year, Pennsylvania completed its North Branch canal extension and linked with the Junction Canal. Coal barges from Pittston, Pennsylvania, soon began making regular trips to Elmira. In 1856 the Lalor Brothers began operating a coal yard built by Charles Cook in Havana. Barges hauling anthracite, bituminous, and semi-bituminous coal directly from the mines unloaded at their yard. The Lalor Brothers sold the coal locally and shipped some to Buffalo, Syracuse, and Oswego, and to their other coal yard in Utica.[31]

Corning and Watkins Glen also benefited from the coal trade. In 1839, a canal boat brought a wood-burning locomotive from Albany to Corning. This locomotive engine launched the Corning-Blossburg Railroad, which brought coal from the mines at Blossburg, Pennsylvania, to be transshipped on the Chemung Canal at Corning.[32] At Watkins Glen, the Morris Run Coal Company constructed

31 *Elmira Gazette*, December 20, 1837, p. 2; Charles Perillo, "The Junction Canal (1855–1871), Elmira, New York, to Athens, Pennsylvania," *Canal History and Technology Proceedings*, vol. 10 (1991), pp. 194–95; *Havana Journal*, November 15, 1856, p. 2.
32 Dimitroff and Janes, *History of the Corning-Painted Post Area*, p. 28.

trestle works to load coal into canal boats at a site along the shore of Seneca Lake called Coal Point. By 1867, the company annually shipped 250,000 tons.[33] Also at Watkins Glen, the Fall Brook Coal Company, founded by John Magee in 1859, established a large facility to transfer coal to canal boats for transport then tow it north on Seneca Lake.[34]

The Corning-Blossburg Railroad, later called the Fall Brook Railroad, hauled the coal to Corning and transshipped it to boats on the Chemung Canal feeder. At Horseheads, the canal barges had their cargoes emptied into coal cars on the Elmira, Jefferson, and Niagara Falls Railroad for the trip to Watkins Glen. At Watkins Glen the coal was loaded onto canal barges once again and towed up Seneca Lake to Geneva. Usually, 10 to 15 large barges, some able to hold 200 tons, were loaded daily.

Magee never liked using the canal route since it closed in the winter, and the Chemung Canal and feeder could not accommodate the larger barges that the Erie used. He found the canal too inefficient and received permission in 1865 to build a short railroad line in Corning, called the Magee Switch, to connect the Corning and Blossburg rail line with the Erie Railroad. This allowed Magee to forego use of the canal completely.[35] The nation's demand for coal outstripped the Chemung Canal's ability to meet it. Railroads could meet the demand for coal year round, and they could do it faster.

While Magee made his fortune from stage lines, railroad construction, and coal, others found the Chemung Canal could launch their fortunes. In fact, the Chemung Canal could boast many success stories. Captain Henry C. Spaulding sold his canal boat in 1841 to engage in lumbering and canal boat manufacturing in Elmira. Eli Wheeler gave up captaining a canal boat and entered the foundry business. His foundry once stood on Lake Street in Elmira. He reputedly built the prototype for the railway sleeping car. Peter Biggs gave up the towpath to manufacture soap in Elmira.[36]

In Havana, Charles Cook certainly exemplified success. He arrived in Havana to help build the Chemung Canal and remained to develop many businesses and institutions in his adopted town. Besides his business enterprises, Cook also built the Episcopal Church and the People's College, a school for which he secured, and later lost, a land grant under the Morrill Act of 1863.

33 "A Visit to the Blossburg Coal Mines," *Elmira Weekly Advertiser*, July 13, p.1867, p. 6.

34 John Magee and Charles Cook joined as partners to build the Erie Railroad from Binghamton to Hornell in the late 1840s. The two men later found themselves as competitors and bitter enemies as each promoted the fortunes of their respective communities, Havana and Watkins Glen. Cook and Magee opposed each other over whether to locate the Schuyler County seat in Watkins or Havana. The two men later squared off in the 1862 election for state senator. Cook won the election after a bitter, vituperative campaign.

35 *History of Tioga County, Pennsylvania* (New York: W.W. Munsel and Company, 1883), p. 41; Joseph C. Boyd, "A Short History of the Fall Brook Railway Co.," February 1957, p. 2, folder on "Fall Brook Railroad," Chemung County Historical Society; *Elmira Gazette*, November 25, 1918, Folder 0640, "Canals," Chemung County Historical Society; *Elmira Weekly Advertiser*, "A Visit to the Blossburg Coal Mines," July 13, 1867, p. 6.

36 Towner, *A History of the Valley and County of Chemung*, pp. 127–28.

This painting of the Chemung Canal passing through the village of Havana (Montour Falls) hangs in the Montour Falls Memorial Library. The brick building on the left is the Montour House, which can still be seen today. The white building with the cupola alongside the canal was known as the Observatory, and like the Montour House, it was owned by Charles Cook. The Observatory burned down on April 25, 1861. (Montour Falls Memorial Library, photo by Lou Cicconi)

Perhaps the most interesting success story about the Chemung Canal also had its origins in Havana. Caleb Hill, a boatman from Havana, had a son named David. David Hill and a friend, Joe Dolph, spent summers tending a lock in Havana. Both young men grew up and studied law. Dolph later moved to Oregon where he was elected to two terms in the U.S. Senate. David Hill also entered politics, served as New York lieutenant governor under Grover Cleveland, and finished Cleveland's term as governor when Cleveland won election to the presidency. Hill then won election to two more terms as governor. After leaving the governor's seat, Hill ran for the U.S. Senate in 1890 and won. On the senate floor, he sat next to his old Chemung Canal friend, Joe Dolph. Now, rather than tending a lock together, they tended to the nation's business.[37]

Not everyone associated with the canal found the social mobility enjoyed by Charles Cook, David Hill, and others. The canal workers more often found themselves trapped in jobs that provided low pay and harsh working conditions.

37 Frank Severne, "Life on the Chemung," *Watkins Express*, December 24, 1952; Morrison, ed. *Early History &c., Havana, New York*, pp. 253–57.

They also faced growing resentment from the middle and upper classes toward the working class.

The commercial boom that gripped the nation resulted in a working class that found itself increasingly alienated from its employers. Wage earners often found themselves no longer working in close proximity to their employers. The upper and middle classes, who witnessed working-class habits, sensed a loss of control. When workers labored under their employer's close tutelage, temperate drinking habits, proper language, and Christianity were encouraged. Greater liberation in the work environment meant employers exerted less control over the workers, but it also meant less employer responsibility for the workers' well-being. Some working-class people drank to excess, used profanity, engaged in fighting, and did not honor the Sabbath. The millennial Christianity that drove the Second Great Awakening, spreading across the nation in the 1830s, believed that the utopian Christian society they hoped to achieve could only occur if society was reformed and purified. The religious movement targeted the working class as a group to be saved, or the entire society would be lost.[38] The Chemung Canal exhibited many symptoms reflecting the growing discord between the upper class and the working class.

The appearance of the Chemung Canal created a population explosion as it attracted people to the area who were seeking opportunity. Many came simply to work on the canal. The canal needed boatmen, boat hands, lockkeepers, and men to build and repair the canal. The population influx redefined the ethnic mix among the population as many Irish workers took their place among the predominantly New England Yankee families who first settled the region.

Before the canal, Elmira, Corning, Horseheads, Havana, and Jefferson (Watkins Glen) were very small communities. The presence of the Chemung Canal changed that. In 1825 Elmira had 1,915 residents. In 1830, when the canal construction began, the population reached 2,950. By 1835 the number had risen to 3,879, and by 1850, after the railroads made their appearance, the census stood at 8,232. The population growth led Thomas Maxwell to remark in 1864, "We have lived to see Elmira, which thirty years ago numbered but her hundreds, and everyone well known, now roll up her ten or twelve thousand, and many of us scarcely know our next neighbor."[39]

The 1830 census for the Town of Erwin (which included the villages of Corning, Lindley, and Caton) reported 974 people. By 1855, the town of Corning alone numbered 6,334, marking a 150 percent increase over the previous 10 years. The village of Corning itself had 3,626 residents in 1855.[40] Big Flats, where the

---

38 Paul Johnson, *Shopkeeper's Millennium* (New York: Hill and Wang, 1978), pp. 6–7, 137–38; Mary Ryan, *Cradle of the Middle Class* (Cambridge: Cambridge University Press, 1981), pp. 11–13; David Roediger, *The Wages of Whiteness* (New York: Verso Publishing, 1991), pp. 50–51.

39 Gordon, *Gazetteer of the State of New York*, 727; "Census of 1830," *Elmira Gazette*, September 18, 1830, p. 2; "Census of Chemung County," *Corning Journal*, December 11, 1850, p. 2; *Elmira Directory of 1863–64*, p. 42.

40 Dimitroff and Janes, *History of the Corning-Painted Post Area*, p. 29, p. 40.

feeder canal passed through from Corning to Horseheads, had 826 residents in 1825, 1,149 in 1830, and by 1850 it reached 1,827. In 1830 Horseheads had 187 residents. Thirty years later it had 1,000.[41]

The numbers alone do not tell the entire story. Many newcomers to the region were Irish immigrants and, as a result, Elmira and Corning developed large Irish populations. The Irish made up the majority of those who constructed the canal and later labored to keep it in repair.

In Elmira, certain neighborhoods began to become characterized as principally Irish. Before 1860 many Irish laborers lived on Elmira's north side in an area known as the "Patch." Later in the century the Irish moved into other areas around the north side and crossed the Chemung River to settle on the south side in neighborhoods called "Pickaway" and "Buttonwoods."[42]

By 1855, 20 percent of the residents of the town of Corning were foreign born. The Irish made up the largest group with 978 living in the township. The check rolls for repairs to the feeder canal published in the *Corning Journal* in 1857 listed many Irish names among the laborers.[43]

The Irish faced discrimination and stereotyping and many locals did not even regard the Irish as racial equals. During the anti-Catholic atmosphere that characterized the 1850s, the Irish church in Corning faced great difficulty acquiring land for a cemetery. After a terrible flood in 1857, a ladies' relief society in Corning decided not to assist any Catholic flood victims. Contemporary local newspapers often contained anecdotes reflecting prejudice towards the Irish. The *Havana Journal* reported in 1853: "Irishmen are very gregarious in their habits. They delight in multitudes, and never take a 'one horse' ride without having the wagon loaded with eight women, fourteen children, the house-dog, and the 'ould joog.'"[44]

The Irish became characterized as drunkards, troublesome, and violent. Incidents occurring on the Chemung Canal sometimes reinforced the stereotypes. The *Havana Republican* reported in 1842: "The whiskey potations in which the Irish laborers employed on the canal below this village freely indulged Sunday evening had the effect to revive all their provincial prejudices towards each other, and finally to produce a fight, in which many of the combatants received bloody noses, and several shantees were torn to the ground."[45]

Two strikes by Irish canal workers demonstrated the prejudice, as well as the fear, the communities harbored toward the Irish. In 1841 Irish workers on

---

41 "Census of Tioga County," *Ithaca Journal*, November 17, 1830, p. 2 (Before 1836, Chemung County was part of Tioga County); "Census of Chemung County," *Corning Journal*, December 11, 1850, p. 2; "Census of 1830," *Elmira Gazette*, September 18, 1830, p. 2; J. H. French, *Gazetteer of the State of New York* (Port Washington, New York: Ira Friedman, Inc., 1860), p. 221.

42 Ellen McTiernan, "Our Melting Pot: Eight Minorities," Folder 135–025, "Ethnic Groups—History of the Irish in Chemung County," Chemung County Historical Society.

43 *Corning Journal*, November 12, 1857, pp. 1–2; Dimitroff and Janes, *History of the Corning-Painted Post Area*, p. 40.

44 Dimitroff and Janes, *History of the Corning-Painted Post Area*, p. 39; *Havana Journal*, November 5, 1853, p. 3; Roediger, *The Wages of Whiteness*, pp. 133–34.

45 *Havana Republican*, February 23, 1842, p. 2.

the Chemung Canal began a strike for higher wages. Havana became alarmed when it learned that disgruntled workers had massed and begun marching along the canal toward the village. The local militia mustered to repel the invasion. An advance party sent to scout the situation discovered that the "enemy" had dispersed and returned to their shanties. The workers were found "quietly eating their breakfasts of codfish and potatoes." It appeared that the militia would not be needed, but at noon a gunshot signaled the need for the militia to reassemble. Townspeople feared that the riot had begun raging once again. The *Havana Republican* reported that the Havana streets were filled with armed men ready "to enforce Yankee rights." While the Irish worried about the possible outcome, the matter ended peacefully when three strike leaders were arrested.[46]

A much larger strike took place on the Chemung Canal in February 1850. The trouble actually began on the Erie Canal and spread to other canals across the state. Irish laborers striking on the Erie Canal near Utica burned a barn belonging to an Erie contractor. Irish workers on the Chemung Canal near Havana decided to instigate their own job action. The unrest centered around dislike for a foreman named Hess. Hess decided that the workers wasted too much time on the job and demanded they work more rigorously. He also believed that the workers were squandering their lives by drinking too much whiskey, so he decided to supply them with plenty of cool, refreshing water while they worked. The workers considered whiskey as part of their wages and resented losing it. They also resented Hess's demand that they work even harder. Inspired by fellow Irish workers on the Erie, the workers decided that something needed to be done and planned a strike.

On February 21 the strike began when Hess got into an argument with an Irish worker, which resulted in a physical confrontation. Hess punched the worker knocking him to the ground, then called a foreman to have the worker taken off the job site. Suddenly, when signaled by others, all the workers dropped what they were doing to pursue Hess, who fled for his life.[47]

The workers put up flyers along the canal work sites that revealed that whiskey, and also rifts among the Irish themselves, were to blame for the riot. Some notices said:

> Let every Connaught and far down man take warning that if
> any of them be found along the canal working after saturday
> night next the grave will be their doom before long and also
> any shanly man that entertains them will share the same
> fate and also any boss that ill uses their men as hess did or

---

46 Ibid., December 8, 1841, p. 2.
47 "Irish Riot on the Chemung Canal," *Havana Republican*, March 8, 1850, Folder 135–025, Chemung County Historical Society; *Havana Journal*, February 16, 1850, p. 2; March 2, 1850, p. 2.

hinders them from drinking or thinks to tyrannize them will suffer immediate death.[48]

The Irish workers resented Hess's water breaks, but they also resented the competition for jobs with the more recent Irish immigrants from Connaught, Ireland. The Irish from Cork were more numerous and made threats against their more recently arrived countrymen, who competed with them for work. On the Erie Canal near Utica, feuding Irish workers attacked one another, resulting in some deaths.

Before they would resume work on the Chemung Canal, the Irish workers demanded better wages, a say in choosing the overseer, and a guarantee that whiskey would be restored. As a response to the strike, one work gang had been fired and work on the canal suspended. The sheriff decided to arrest the strike ringleaders. He arrived early one morning with a small posse only to be outnumbered by the Irish workers wielding shovels and tools as weapons. The sheriff returned in the afternoon with 65 men armed with muskets. When it appeared he had the situation under control and the ringleaders taken into custody, the sheriff left the scene to catch the train back to Elmira.

After the sheriff left, an Irishman named Hickey appeared and rallied the workers in opposition to the arrests. A melee broke out when the Irish laborers attacked the posse with clubs, shovels, and stones. The outnumbered posse fled, allowing some prisoners to escape in the confusion. On March 2 a militia detachment from Elmira arrived to quell the insurrection. With that the strike ended. The prisoners taken were questioned and released when authorities realized they had little evidence against them.[49]

The response to the strikes demonstrated the townspeople's fear and dislike of the Irish, but the same fears and dislikes were often directed at the canal working class in general. Many people regarded the boatmen and boat hands on the canal as contemptible individuals who swore, drank, and fought their way along the canal. The place names given to some locations along the Chemung Canal reflect the regard people had for the canal culture. The basin at Gibson where canal boats could load and unload became known as "Suckerville." Croton, a small community north of Millport, earned the nickname "Ratville." Both places had a reputation for harboring many unsavory characters.[50]

Boatmen became involved in counterfeiting rings, rapes, murders, and fights. Boat captain Thomas Crandall of Corning was arrested in 1859 for passing counterfeit money. Authorities arrested boatman Ransom Barton in Havana

48 *Havana Journal*, March 2, 1850, p. 2.
49 "Trouble With the Irish," Havana Journal, March 2, 1850, p. 2; "The Havana Riot and the Sheriff," *Elmira Republican*, March 15, 1850, p. 2; *Havana Republican*, March 8, 1850, Folder 135–025, Chemung County Historical Society; *Elmira Republican*, March 8, 1850, excerpt from the *Utica Observer*, p. 2.
50 Earle McGowan to J. M. Norris, November 15, 1968, Folder on "Canals," Schuyler County Historical Society; "Detective Sketches, Eight Years Secret Service," *Elmira Sunday Telegram*, October 25, 1888, p. 2. This article was about the exploits of a detective who tracked down counterfeiters and horse thieves in New York and Pennsylvania.

in 1860 for committing a rape in Elmira. G. F. Harris, a canal boat captain for the Bennet and Randall Lumber Company in Elmira, cashed a check for tolls and expenses he was supposed to deliver to the toll collector at Horseheads and then ran off with the money.[51]

Several merchants and businessmen wrote to the canal commissioners in 1834 seeking permission to pay the tolls on their shipments for the entire canal system at the collector's office in Horseheads or Havana. The men complained that the boatmen were frequently unreliable in handling the money for the tolls. The letter explained that the businessmen had "experienced much inconvenience and in some instances considerable pecuniary loss in being obliged to entrust irresponsible boatmen with sufficient money to pay their tolls through the different canals."[52]

Canal men also developed a reputation for fighting. Millport, considered the center for canal operations along the Chemung Canal, attracted young men from miles around seeking to test their manhood by demonstrating their fighting prowess against the canal men. Captain Newton Baker, a boatman from Pennsylvania who often navigated the Chemung Canal, recalled: "The boatmen up that way didn't think much of us Pennsylvanians and there was often fights. One time there was a fight at Horseheads and a fellow knocked my Uncle Wesley down the bank."[53]

Canal boatmen had a reputation for being dishonest. Theft and deceit abounded along the canal. Canal boat crews often committed petty theft from the cargo they carried, from property owners adjoining the canal, and even from each other. Barrels with rum, whiskey, or molasses sometimes had their iron hoops pounded down so that a hole could be drilled into them, allowing the boatmen to sample the merchandise. After plugging the hole, they pounded the hoop back over the barrel to cover their theft.

Boatmen also often helped themselves to chickens roosting in tree branches hanging over the canal towpath. A long pole with a wire crook at the end would be used to snatch the chickens from the limbs. When transporting a cargo on the canal, boatmen had to keep guard all night to prevent other boatmen from stealing goods from their boat. It is little wonder that one boat captain was led to comment, "Some persons seemed to think us boatmen were a light-fingered lot."[54]

The men and boys who worked on the canal were also known for their bad language. The *Havana Journal* reported in 1853 that there were 30,000 men and 7,000 boys employed on the state canals and "enough cursing and swearing to

51 The Corning Journal, May 5, 1859, p. 3; *Havana Journal*, September 8, 1860, p. 2; July 28, 1855, p. 2.
52 Letter to the Board of Canal Commissioners from Businessmen of Havana and Elmira, March, 1834, New York State Archives.
53 Louis Tomlinson, "The Chemung Canal System," excerpt from the *Elmira Sunday Telegram*, c. 1870; From the reminiscences of Captain G. Newton Baker, folder CF 060–045, Chemung County Historical Society.
54 Hazel McGowan to Earl McGowan, November 15, 1968, folder on "Canals," Schuyler County Historical Society. Hazel McGowan's maternal grandmother was adopted by a canal boatman and his wife. The letter related some of her reminiscences of the Chemung Canal; Diary of Gilbert Hillerman (from Reading Center), who captained a canal boat on the Chemung and Erie Canals, May 10, 1853, Schuyler County Historical Society. Hillerman discusses how

dam Niagara." That same year the *Havana Journal* echoed the concern of another newspaper that "profane swearing dishonors God, degrades the swearer, and corrupts the whole moral nature. It is the shame of civilization, and the shame of any people among whom it prevails." Some young men in Elmira even formed an anti-swearing society in 1867. It is doubtful that many members of their group worked on the canal.[55]

One canal boat owner had to petition the Canal Board to change the name of his boat due to the language he confronted while navigating the Chemung Canal. P. J. Velie had lived in Pine Valley and operated his boat, the *G. W. Moorhouse of Pine Valley*, on the Chemung Canal. He moved his boat to a town called Oramel on the Genesee Valley Canal in 1854, and he wished to rechristen his boat *The Olean of Oramel*. Velie explained that he wished to change the name because when operating on the Chemung Canal, "the similitudes of 'Moorhouse' to 'Whorehouse' has occasioned him much annoyance from rude people, while navigating on the canals with said boat." The board granted the name change.[56]

Another criticism about the men working on the Chemung Canal concerned their drinking habits: they were hard drinkers. Like those who built the canal, the men who worked to keep the canal in repair were served whiskey on the job. Canal boat captains often drank as they guided their boats through the canal. On many occasions, alcohol abuse led to crime and tragedy.

Some canal workers drowned after they became intoxicated and fell into the canal. In November 1849, an Irish worker named Hickey fell into the canal near Havana and drowned. The coroner's report and witnesses said that intoxication contributed to Hickey's death. In 1860 canal boat captain Decatur Patronne also drowned when he fell into the canal due to intoxication.[57] Contemporary newspapers often reported bodies found in the canal. In many instances, alcohol contributed to the drowning.

Alcohol also led to a canal murder in Gibson in 1857. Along the canal were many groceries that boatmen and their families frequented as they traveled the canal. Boatman Thomas Edger, after working on the canal all day, decided to visit the grocery at Gibson owned by Jerome McBain. Edger hoped to pick up some whiskey on credit. McBain sold Edger the whiskey but refused to let him have sugar on credit. The two men argued. Edger became so enraged that he grabbed McBain by the throat. McBain broke away and ran to the rear of the store where he kept a gun. McBain fired one shot, striking Edger in the head and killing him instantly. Both men were intoxicated at the time, which meant they had been

he had to stay up the entire night to watch his freight, which was a large load of flour; from the reminiscences of Captain G. Newton Baker, folder CF 060–045, Chemung County Historical Society. Baker transported coal from Pennsylvania to New York City using the Chemung and Erie Canals.

55 *Havana Journal*, June 25, 1853, p. 3; October 29, 1853, p. 1; *Elmira Weekly Advertiser*, June 22, 1861, p. 3.
56 P. J. Velie to the Canal Department of the State of New York, March 13, 1854. Series A1440, Box 2, 922, New York State Archives.
57 *Havana Journal*, November 3, 1849, p. 2; August 11, 1860, p. 2.

drinking while they worked. The sheriff arrested McBain and sent him to jail in Bath.[58]

In 1850 Dr. G. D. Bailey from Havana complained about the Irish workers engaged in repairs along the canal. Bailey's property suffered as men ruined his fences and cut timber on his land. Armed workers sometimes chased Bailey off his own property when he confronted them. In May, Dr. Bailey directed his 17-year-old brother, Horace, to demolish a shanty on his property that the Irish workers had used and abandoned. While Horace Bailey was tearing down the shanty, some Irish workers who disliked Dr. Bailey showed up and confronted Horace. Three powerfully built Irishmen, all of whom were said to be intoxicated, began making menacing advances towards the young Bailey. Frightened, Horace Bailey drew a revolver. The three men continued to advance. Two of them, Andrew Sullivan and Sinan Hickey, began to strike Bailey, who fired his pistol in self-defense. Sullivan fell dead, shot through the heart. Hickey continued to hit Bailey. Bailey fired again, killing Hickey. The third man tried to attack Bailey only to be restrained by onlookers who had rushed to the scene. Bailey was arrested and taken to Elmira. A canal boatman testified that shortly before the attack he heard Sullivan threaten to kill Horace Bailey. After questioning, authorities discharged Bailey on the grounds that he acted in self-defense.[59]

With all the drinking, fighting, dishonesty, and swearing exhibited by the canal men, local communities took efforts to encourage canal laborers to attend church and mend their ways. Religion became an attempt to control the excesses exhibited by the working class. A chief concern among the local canal communities centered around observing the Sabbath. Canal traffic, however, did not stop for religious reasons. The market economy demanded that goods and resources be delivered as quickly as possible. Canal boat captains, lockkeepers, and others who worked on the canal did not usually attend the local churches. Many community members resented such disregard for the Sabbath.

In 1837 the *Elmira Gazette* published the resolutions passed at a religious meeting held in Southport. According to the "Resolutions of the Presbytery of Chemung," God intended the Sabbath as a day to be kept holy, and wanton destruction awaited societies that failed to do so. Members present at the meeting proclaimed that those who ran their boats or barges on the Sabbath for personal gain or convenience "disregard the authority of God, trample on his law, and profane the day of rest." The resolution urged other churches to discipline their members who desecrated the Sabbath.[60]

Over 20 years later, the Sabbath issue still persisted. The *Corning Journal* printed an excerpt from the *Penn Yan Democrat* that condemned operating canals on Sunday. Both Penn Yan and Corning were canal towns. The Crooked Lake

---

58 *Corning Journal*, November 12, 1857, p. 3; November 19, 1857, p.3; *Havana Journal*, November 21, 1857, p. 2.
59 *Havana Journal*, May 4, 1850, p. 2; May 11, 1850, p. 2; May 25, 1850, p.2.
60 *Elmira Gazette*, February 11, 1837, p. 2.

Canal, which connected Keuka (Crooked) Lake and Seneca Lake, began in Penn Yan. The editorial, entitled "The Sabbath and the Canals," argued that closing the locks and canal business on the Sabbath would promote better work and better morals among the lock tenders and boatmen. The editorial said: "We believe it would improve the character of lock tenders and boatmen on the Canals of the State . . . . To the canals the advantage would be an introduction of a better class of men upon them, by making transportation on them safer and property committed to them more secure."[61]

Although some people expressed fear that a day off would only give the canal workers more free time for debauchery, the editorial stated confidently that good would conquer evil. More boatmen would spend the Sabbath reading, attending church, and improving their minds. In any event, the editorial clearly shows that lock tenders and boatmen did not have a reputation in the community for good moral character.

The editorial took the stance that the Sabbath issue required government involvement. Other businesses were required by law to cease operations on Sunday, so why not canals? Since the canals belonged to the state, did not the state have a right to make rules about managing its property? Did not the state have a duty to promote the public good? The demand for legislation to enforce the Sabbath showed that the churches and the local populace lacked the coercive power to reform the canal men, just as attempts by temperance groups had failed to curb the working class thirst for spirits.[62] The editorial did not bring the change it sought. Canals continued to operate on Sunday.

Although the churches found they could not persuade canal workers to obey the Sabbath and refrain from alcohol, employers found they could exercise coercive power over the canal men in politics. Although often described as free labor, wage laborers frequently found that they lacked freedom in the polling place. Contractors sometimes used coercion to influence the votes of the canal workers. In 1859 local newspapers reported accusations that Charles Breed, the repair contractor for the Chemung Canal, pressured the lock tenders and those employed under him to vote the Democratic ticket. With the secret ballot still a distant reality, employers could easily keep tabs on their workers' voting habits. Those workers who defied the employer's wishes faced being publicly fired at the polls.[63]

Political parties also used the Chemung Canal as a means to get votes. A key state issue in the late 1840s involved an attempt in the state legislature to gain approval for enlarging the Erie Canal and the lateral canals to allow more traffic and bigger barges. The Whig Party supported internal improvements, and the

61 "The Sabbath and the Canals," excerpt from the *Penn Yan Democrat*, Corning Journal, April 1, 1858, p. 2.
62 Ibid.; Johnson, *A Shopkeeper's Millennium*, 83–84.
63 *Havana Journal*, November 12, 1859, p. 2.

Havana Journal exhorted canal workers to do their duty for the Whig Party in 1849:

> Every BOATMAN and LABORER should so arrange his business as to be at the place where he has a legal right to vote on the day of election . . . . Retain the Whigs, whose zeal, faithfulness and skillful management have been proved, and the capacity of the canals will be increased FIFTY PER CENT . . . . Let not the enemies of the public works triumph through the indifference of those who should be their firmest friends. Let every "Canaller" be at his post on the morning of the SIXTH.[64]

In 1851 the *Havana Journal* reprinted an article from the *Rochester Democrat* urging canal men to vote Whig. It reminded the workers "that the Whig Policy will give employment to THOUSANDS OF LABORING MEN through the winter months, the very time when they most need it, and the Locofoco policy would deprive them of it . . . . The interests of the State, of the Laboring Men and of the Whig Party, are the same."[65]

Prejudice toward the Irish often waned prior to elections as rival parties courted the vote of the workingman. During the Chemung Canal strike in February 1850, the *Elmira Gazette* referred to the striking workers as "ignorant Irishmen." A rival newspaper, the *Elmira Republican,* explained to their readers that the *Gazette* editor's prejudice toward the Irish would vanish with the next election. Referring to the elections scheduled for the following year, the *Republican* wrote, "Who does not know that before that time these 'ignorant' Irishmen will become highly *intelligent* democratic voters?"[66]

An anecdote in a contemporary newspaper helps sum up the predicament faced by canal workers. An Irishman, operating a huge windlass used to hoist stone from canal boats, remarked that the machine seemed to be a fine instrument able to do the work of ten men, but they would have a devil of a time getting it to vote.[67]

In the final assessment, the Chemung Canal did bring tremendous economic growth to the local area. It launched new industries, established a cash economy, increased consumption, and expanded the population. The canal brought economic opportunities and prosperity; however, it also brought changes that local people did not predict. The canal created tension between the working class and the local populace as alcohol abuse, crime, and strikes threatened stabil-

64 Ibid., November 3, 1849, p. 2.
65 Ibid., excerpt from the *Rochester Democrat,* October 31, 1851, p. 2.
66 "The Havana Riot and the Sheriff," *Elmira Republican*, March 15, 1850, p. 2
67 *Havana Journal*, November 4, 1854, p. 3.

ity. It created problems about ethnicity as the numerous Irish immigrants faced prejudice and discrimination.

The changes the canal nurtured paved the way for the future. The market economy continued to grow, and the canal helped feed it until a better way displaced it. The railroad would prove that its abilities exceeded the canal in moving resources, people, and goods. Competition with railroads would doom the Chemung Canal, but the canal also contributed to its own demise.

CHAPTER FOUR

An Unfortunate Limb of
Our Commercial Tree

THE THREE MAJOR REASONS THAT EXPLAIN THE SHORT LIFE of the Chemung Canal were costly repairs, the railroads, and the failure to enlarge the canal. Competition with the railroads was the primary reason the Chemung Canal closed its gates for good in 1878. The canal could not match the speed and versatility the railroads offered. The market economy the canal helped develop demanded more goods and faster delivery. Business increasingly turned to the railroads rather than the inefficient canals, which closed every winter.

Despite the railroads' obvious advantages, the transition from canals to railroads did not happen immediately. In fact, railroads first brought the Chemung Canal its greatest prosperity as they operated in conjunction with one another. Only when rail lines proliferated and became safer did their advantages overtake the canal.

The railroads alone do not explain the canal's decline. The canal never actually proved very profitable. Expenses more often exceeded the toll revenue as flood damages, decaying locks, and silting necessitated costly repairs. As expenses mounted, the canal became a liability the public could no longer afford.

The failure to enlarge the Chemung Canal, which would have enabled it to accommodate larger barges and allowed it to compete with the railroads, also contributed to its declining usefulness. Public ownership meant that politicians, in the attempt to keep taxes down, showed little willingness to fund enlargement or more durable locks for the Chemung Canal.

Before the railroads arrived, the public tolerated the expensive upkeep for the canal since it enjoyed a virtual monopoly for shipping goods in bulk. From its inception in 1833 until the late 1840s, the Chemung Canal did not have to contend with any competition from railroads. That changed when the New York and Erie Railroad arrived in Elmira in October 1849. Two months later the Chemung Railroad began operation. The Chemung Railroad ran parallel to the Chemung Canal from Elmira to Watkins Glen and later joined with the New York Central Railroad. The Erie Railroad crossed the southern New York counties from Dunkirk to New York City.[1]

Having these railroads available did not initiate a sudden desertion from the Chemung Canal. Although railroads had tremendous potential, there were three reasons why they did not instantly knock the Chemung Canal and the other lateral canals from their commercial pedestal. First of all, the early railroads did not have a good reputation for safety. Newspapers from the 1850s reported many terrible train wrecks that killed or maimed people. When the *Havana Journal* reported the suggestion that railroad companies might reduce their fares and still realize a good profit, the newspaper wryly noted that having more passengers would "keep a supply of easily acquired funds on hand to pay for those whom they expect to kill."[2]

The Chemung Canal also had hazards, but they did not approach the dangers a railroad presented. Speed never became a problem on the canal since the boats moved at a snail's pace while towed through the water. Drowning reigned as the biggest hazard on the canal. In 1854 Cornelius Ryan, the lock tender for lock 24 in Millport, fell into his lock and drowned. Sedate Dibble, the lock tender for lock number one at Havana, fell into the lock in 1856 when he was tripped by the tow line of a canal boat. He was crushed against the wall of the lock by the canal boat and left an invalid for the rest of his life. In 1847 Silas Downing, keeper of lock number three, opened the gate to let water out of the lock when he fell in. His nine-year-old son stretched out his hand to save his father, only to be pulled in as well. Both drowned as a result.[3]

Children playing near the canal locks flirted with danger. Occasionally, they took risks that proved fatal. The Chemung Canal was an inviting place to cool off on a hot summer day. Boys swimming near locks sometimes jumped onto loaded boats as the boats passed into the locks. In 1854, a fourteen-year-old boy jumped onto a canal barge loaded with timber as it entered lock five near Havana. The barge bumped against the side of the lock as he landed on it, and the boy lost his balance. When he fell into the lock, the barge, with its many tons of cargo, crushed him to death against the side of the lock.[4]

Jackson Hodge, a steersman on the canal boat *Edward C. Miles*, has the unfortunate distinction of being the victim of perhaps the most bizarre accident on the Chemung Canal. According to a newspaper account, Hodge stood holding the rudder handle of his boat as it headed south on the canal only a mile and a half

1 *Havana Journal*, December 8, 1849, p. 2.
2 *Havana Journal*, July 30, 1853, p. 2.
3 *Havana Journal*, June 10, 1854, p. 2; May 24, 1856, p. 2; October 14, 1854, p. 2; August 11, 1860; Morrison, ed., *Early History, &c., Havana, New York*, excepted from the *Havana Republican*, p. 344.
4 *Havana Journal*, June 3, 1854, p. 2.

from Horseheads on August 18, 1867. A terrible thunder storm had begun to rage. While standing at his post, a powerful bolt of lightning struck Hodge on his head, killing him instantly. It burned a stripe down his body from his left shoulder to his hip. The current passed through the tiller he was leaning against and exited out the bottom of the boat. The caulking in the boat was removed in a large area, and the boat had to be put into dry dock for repairs. Half of Hodge's felt hat had been burned up, and so had the hair and beard on the left side of his face. Others on the boat, who had been below deck at the time, were completely unhurt.[5]

The canal was not without hazards, but overall the hazards posed by canals were slight compared to the dangers railroads posed to passengers. Since the Chemung Canal served chiefly as a freight canal and not a passenger service, shipping goods rather than people was the real issue in the battle with the railroads. Railroads faced a second drawback as goods could be shipped more cheaply by canal than by rail. Even by 1860, the ton-per-mile rates on the Erie Canal averaged nearly one dollar less than the rates available on the Erie Railroad. From 1850 to 1900, the average ton-per-mile rates on the New York Central and Erie Railroads could not equal the rates available on the canals.[6]

Many people believed that preserving the canals, even though they were expensive to maintain, helped to keep railroad rates from becoming excessive. If the canals closed, some feared the railroads would become a monopoly and raise their rates. A businessman wrote to John Arnot, the Junction Canal president, when he learned the Junction Canal and Union Canal might close. The businessman wished to sell his quarries near Philadelphia, but the buyers feared that without the canals they could not afford to ship their products. Shipping costs could make or break a business. When the Chemung Canal closed in 1878, the pottery works in Havana had to close because it could not afford shipping New Jersey clay to their worksite by rail.[7]

A third reason why railroads did not immediately supplant the Chemung Canal can be blamed on inadequate railroad mileage. With only a few rail lines in existence the railroads could not challenge the canal. In fact, the early railroads depended upon the canals. Without enough connecting lines, the railroads relied on the canal system to deliver goods to locations not serviced by railroads. Rather than hurt business, the local railroads actually increased business on the Chemung Canal. The Chemung Canal had a peak year in 1854, thanks to the added business the railroads brought to its waters. The freight that passed through the canal that year climbed to over 270,000 tons, an amount higher than

5 *Elmira Weekly Advertiser*, August 24, 1867, p. 4.
6 Spiro Patton, "Canals in American Business and Economic History: A Review of the Issues," *Canal History and Technology Proceedings*, vol. IV (March 28, 1987): p. 9.
7 Ibid.; A. Barton Hepburn, *Artificial Waterways and Commercial Development* (New York: MacMillan Company, 1909), pp. 46–47, 104; Morrison, ed., *Early History, &c., Havana, New York*, 226; A. Overfield to John Arnot, October 22, 1868, Arnot Family Papers, Chemung County Historical Society; *Elmira Weekly Advertiser*, March 31, 1859, p. 6; "The State Canals," *Elmira Weekly Advertiser*, October 5, 1867, p. 2.

Habana Journal.

CIRCULATION 1100.

SATURDAY, JUNE 20, 1857.

Great Freshet.

On Wednesday evening last our place was visited with the most destructive freshet ever known among us; the damage to gardens, fences, side-walks and property is very large —no lives lost, and no buildings removed, but scarcely a milldam is left on the stream south of us. The farms and fences up the valley have suffered great damage, and the Chemung Canal, from this place to the summit level, a distance of eight miles, is literally torn in pieces. We understand the Resident Engineer in charge says that it will take from four to six weeks, even with good weather, before it can again be navigable for boats. The village of Millport has suffered severely; several buildings were swept away by the flood, and a large amount of damage done besides property destroyed. It is said there was considerable damage done at Elmira, but we have not heard the particulars. At Gibson the hotel was undermined by the stream passing near it and carried into the canal on the opposite side of the street; the barns belonging to the hotel were also swept away; a part of the State dam across the Chemung river at this place is gone; a piece of the towing-path to the canal near the dam is also gone, and a portion of the river continues to run down the canal. At Corning a very large amount of property was destroyed, buildings carried away, and it is also said that two lives were lost. The village of Monterey has also suffered considerable damage, and the plank road from that place to Coopers Plains is more or less injured. The road down Post creek from Ostrander's mills is impassible, and travelers have

Nearly every season witnessed flooding that caused destruction to the canal. One of the worst floods occurred in June 1857. Fast-moving water crashed through Millport, sending the residents fleeing to the hilltops. The flood greatly damaged the Chemung Canal as it washed away towpaths and embankments. Nearly all the communities along the canal suffered from the ravages of the flood. The *Havana Journal* reported the devastation. (*Havana Journal*, Montour Falls Memorial Library)

any previous year. The tolls collected exceeded $21,000 and would not be equaled again until the Civil War injected renewed life into the canal.[8]

Together the railroads and the canal brought prosperity to Corning. The Blossburg and Corning Railroad brought Pennsylvania coal to Corning to be transshipped on the Chemung Canal. The Erie Railroad brought carloads of logs and lumber from the western counties of Allegany and Cattaraugus to be loaded onto canal boats in Corning. Corning became a valuable inland port that at one time ranked among the five busiest canal ports in New York State.[9]

After the Civil War the railroads became the major freight carrier, thanks to more rail lines. Before 1868, the canals still hauled over half the freight tonnage in New York State.[10] Yet competition from railroads caused the canal commission to respond in the 1850s. During that decade the New York canals began experiencing a decline in tonnages carried, and that also meant a decline in revenues. To compete with the railroads, the canal commission realized they needed to reduce rates and enlarge the canal bed to accommodate bigger barges.

Before 1847, railroads in New York State often could only haul freight when the canals closed for the winter. From 1847 to 1851, the railroads could carry freight year-round, but they had to pay tolls for carrying freight during the canal season. After 1851, the railroads were freed from paying tolls, and the canals had to lower their rates or face losing business to the railroads. In 1850 the Chemung Canal handled 128,263 tons of goods yet collected nearly $16,000 in tolls. In 1856 the canal hauled over 245,000 tons yet realized only $17,000 in tolls. Two years later, 205,000 tons were shipped, producing only $16,000 in toll revenue. Tonnage on the Chemung Canal kept increasing, but revenues declined as tolls were lowered due to railroad competition.[11]

As canal revenues fell throughout the 1850s, more tax dollars had to be dedicated to keeping the state canals in repair since the toll revenue did not yield enough.[12] The public had to consider whether the publicly owned canals should be protected from the private property of the railroad corporations. The rising expense for maintaining the Chemung Canal and the other lateral canals eventually made them a liability the public showed no willingness to bear. Unfortunately, an amendment added to the state constitution in 1846 had declared the state canals to be property permanently belonging to the state. Despite public dissatisfaction over rising canal expenditures, the state felt compelled to preserve and protect its property against the privately owned railroads.[13]

8 Whitford, *History of the Canal System*, pp. 1062–65.
9 "Port of Corning," *Corning Journal*, April 29, 1853, p. 2.
10 Hepburn, *Artificial Waterways and Commercial Development*, p. 104.
11 Whitford, *History of the Canal System*, pp. 1062–1065; "Tolling Railroads," *Elmira Weekly Advertiser*, March 31, 1859, p. 6; Hepburn, *Artificial Waterways and Commercial Development*, p. 103; Sheriff, *The Artificial River*, p. 173; "Trade and Tonnage of the Canals," report of the canal department auditor to the New York State legislature, *Havana Journal*, February 17, 1855, p. 2.
12 Hepburn, *Artificial Waterways and Commercial Development*, 103; "Trade and Tonnage of the Canals," report of the canal department auditor to the New York State legislature, *Havana Journal*, February 17, 1855, p. 2.
13 Whitford, *History of the Canal System*, pp. 637, 766.

The guard lock at Gibson let the water in from the Chemung River to the feeder canal. A dam on the river created a pool of water used to supply most of the water for the Chemung Canal. The photograph was taken around 1870. (Chemung County Historical Society)

The expensive repairs the Chemung Canal required contributed to its eventual downfall. Flood repairs became the biggest expense. Nearly every year brought destructive flooding that damaged the canal. Its location adjacent to many streams made damages almost a certainty any time high water struck. Many floods wreaked havoc on the canal, but the worst floods happened in 1857.

In June 1857 the *Corning Journal* reported that heavy rains had fallen for 10 days. By June 17, the local rivers and streams swelled to levels higher than many residents could recall. The raging waters wreaked devastation all along the canal. At Gibson, where the feeder canal began, a creek had risen to a rushing torrent that swept a hotel building into the canal. The creek also cut into the canal tow-path and then into the Chemung River. As a result, the river began emptying into the canal, carrying sediment into the canal prism. The swollen river current also severely damaged the feeder dam.[14]

Big Flats reported that the feeder canal had sustained much damage as canal embankments gave way to the flood waters. Elmira also reported much damage. In Havana, the flood waters reached the first floor of Charles Cook's Montour House even though it stood elevated several feet above street level. The flood destroyed 4,573 feet of towpath along the entire canal.[15]

Millport suffered the worst. The canal could not handle all the water running into it. To protect the canal, water had to be let out of it. The increased volume this created in Catharine Creek added to the disaster. The creek became a torrent sending a wall of water downstream that swept away everything in its path. The flood carried off houses, barns, mill dams, and mills. Millport residents fled to nearby hills to escape the disaster.[16]

More than 500 men immediately set to work repairing the damaged canal. Although local newspapers expressed hope that the canal would quickly reopen, repair efforts slowed due to more wet weather. On June 30 another heavy rainfall caused more high water that carried away many repairs that had been done. Finally, on July 19 the canal reopened.[17]

Mother Nature had not finished, however. More heavy rains produced yet another flood on November 9. This flood proved even more destructive than the one in June. Fortunately for the Chemung Canal, the recent repairs had strengthened the canal and protected it from severe damage. Corning received the worst damage from this flood. Many homes had water up to the windows and rooftops. The flood ruined the guard lock at Gibson and badly damaged the feeder dam once again. Although the canal had weathered the flood, it had to close navigation until December 3 because the feeder canal could not supply water to the canal due to the damages at Gibson. The repairs necessitated by the floods in 1857 proved

14 *Corning Journal*, June 18, 1857, p. 3; *Havana Journal*, June 20, 1857, p. 2.
15 Whitford, *History of the Canal System*, 632; *Corning Journal*, June 25, 1857, p. 2.
16 H. B. Pierce and D. Hamilton Hurd, *History of Tioga, Chemung, Tompkins, and Schuyler Counties, New York* (Philadelphia: Everts and Ensign, 1879), p. 361; Towner, *History of the Valley and County of Chemung*, p. 548.
17 *Havana Journal*, June 27, 1857, p. 2; July 11, 1857, p. 2; *Annual Report of the Canal Commissioners*, 1858, p.72.

costly. Even before the November flood struck, over $87,000 had been needed to repair the canal.[18]

The 1857 floods exemplified the destructive force that floods wielded over the canal. Other bad floods that caused extensive damages to the canal occurred in 1850 and 1861. In 1865 a flood nearly demolished the feeder dam near Corning.[19] Thanks to deforestation, greater cultivation, and increased settlement nearly every year occasioned flood damages that required many expensive repairs.

While too much water often menaced the canal, too little water also presented a constant hindrance. The Chemung River served as the main water source for the canal, and often it could not provide enough. Dry periods in the summer months created headaches for boat crews and lockkeepers trying to get boats through the canal. Silting in the prism and locks added to the problem, making it difficult for boats to get enough draft. Although engineers made suggestions for solving the problem, the low water-level nuisance was never adequately addressed.[20]

By 1856 the water supply issue became more crucial. The Junction Canal would soon begin operations and it, too, would rely on the Chemung River for its water supply. Local businessmen endorsed enlarging the Chemung Canal to allow for larger barges. Other canals, such as the Junction Canal and the Erie Canal, could accommodate larger barges. It was troublesome to transship goods from a large boat to a smaller boat so the goods could pass through the Chemung Canal. Canal business had been steadily increasing in the early 1850s, and enlargement would improve the canal's ability to meet the increased demands and counter the railroad competition. Yet, enlargement would create a wider and deeper canal prism, requiring the need for an even larger water supply to meet the increased demand. Pennsylvanians were already complaining about the low water level in the Chemung River due to the diversion of water for the Chemung Canal. Mill owners along the canal frequently complained that the canal denied them sufficient water to maintain their businesses.

Canal Commissioner Henry Fitzhugh underscored the problem in a letter to engineer O. C. Hartwell in 1856. Fitzhugh wrote: "The entire waters of the Chemung River are quite insufficient for the supply of the canal during the dry portion of the year . . . . A greater supply must be obtained, or navigation will have to be entirely suspended during the dry season of the year."[21] How could the Chemung Canal get more water? Fitzhugh suggested that Hartwell investigate

18 *Corning Journal*, November 12, 1857, p.2; *Annual Report of the Canal Commissioners*, 1858, p. 73, p. 78.
19 *Annual Report of the Canal Commissioners*, 1851, pp. 51–52; Ibid., 1862, p. 79; Ibid., 1866, p. 48.
20 *Annual Report of the Canal Commissioners*, 1871, p. 98; Canal Commissioner Henry Fitzhugh to O. C. Hartwell, Division Engineer, November 11, 1856, excerpt from the *Annual Report of the Canal Commissioners*, 1857, p. 84.
21 Canal Commissioner Henry Fitzhugh to O. C. Hartwell, Division Engineer, November 11, 1856, excerpt from the *Annual Report of the Canal Commissioners*, 1857, p. 84; Petitions to the Canal Board and those reported in the Assembly Journals identify many mill owners along the canal seeking damages for losses when the Chemung Canal denied them sufficient water; see *Assembly Documents*, 1841, "Petition of Robert Land and Others," p. 170, New York State Library; *Assembly Documents*, 1841, "Petition of Harvey Luce," p. 47; *Assembly Documents*, 1840, "Petition of John Nichols [et. al.]," p. 327.

using two small lakes, Mud Lake and Little Lake (Waneta and Lamoka Lakes), located between Seneca Lake and Keuka Lake. Hartwell inspected the lakes and reported back to Fitzhugh that the two lakes would make excellent reservoirs that would give the Chemung Canal a plentiful water supply. Although Hartwell gave a favorable report, it did not result in any action.[22] The expensive repairs necessitated by the 1857 floods, and the crumbling locks on the canal, which required immediate attention, doomed the chances for any expenditures to create extra reservoirs. The water shortage continued to be a problem. In one instance, all the water that could be saved from the Chemung River for several weeks still proved insufficient to keep the canal running.[23]

Even when the canal did have enough water, another severe problem often interrupted canal traffic. Flooding and erosion deposited silt in the canal prism, which sometimes made the canal impassable for the heavily laden boats. Boats often became stuck in the four-foot-deep canal and in the locks.[24]

The lake level from lock one at Havana to Seneca Lake became the worst area for silt deposits. From the canal's opening until 1849, this section was a continual annoyance for boatmen. Boatman Alexander Clauharty from Havana testified to the canal commissioners that the sandbars in the lake level were so bad that boats had to pole their way through and even had to build makeshift dams to get enough water to pass over the bars. The state had to employ men to act as "lighters" along the route. They would unload boat cargoes onto wagons to lighten the load, allowing the boats to navigate the shallow waterway.[25]

The decision by Holmes Hutchinson to use Catharine Creek to carry the canal boats from Havana to Seneca Lake led to the lake-level problem. The creek constantly filled in with silt. Every year workmen were kept busy dredging the creek bed to keep boats moving. Every season men using teams of horses had to drag an underwater excavator to remove deposits in the creek. It became a Sisyphean task. As soon as they cleared one sandbar, a new one formed elsewhere.[26] The creek had to be abandoned as the canal route and a completely artificial waterway was constructed from Havana to the lake. The legislature appropriated the funds in 1848, and workmen completed the work by 1850. For the first time in years, fully loaded boats navigated from lock one to Seneca Lake without hindrance.[27]

While extending the canal from Havana to Seneca Lake solved the silting problem, another chronic problem did not have such an easy solution. Ever since

22 Canal Commissioner Henry Fitzhugh to O. C. Hartwell, Division Engineer, November 11, 1856; O. C. Hartwell to Canal Commissioner Henry Fitzhugh, January 4, 1857, excerpt from the *Annual Report of the Canal Commissioners, 1857*, p. 84.
23 Whitford, *History of the Canal System*, p. 632.
24 *Annual Report of the Canal Commissioners*, 1853, p. 89.
25 *Havana Journal*, April 20, 1850, p. 4; *Annual Report of the Canal Commissioners*, 1837, p. 41; Ibid., 1838, p. 29; Ibid., 1845, pp. 56–57; Whitford, *History of the Canal System*, p. 626.
26 Whitford, *History of the Canal System*, p. 626; *Assembly Documents*, no. 141, March 5, 1845, "Report of the Canal Board on the petition of John Bump for relief," p. 1. Bump filed a claim for compensation for one of his horses, which was injured while pulling a boat through Catharine Creek in 1844.
27 Whitford, *History of the Canal System*, 626–28; *Annual Report of the Canal Commissioners*, 1845, pp. 66–67; Ibid., 1849, p. 69; Ibid., 1851, pp. 52–53; *Assembly Documents*, no. 141, March 5, 1845, "Report of the Canal Board on the petition of John Bump for relief," p. 1.

Lock 49, more commonly known as the spillway lock, was located near Water Street in Elmira. It allowed excess water to run out of the Chemung Canal and into the Chemung River. Originally the spillway lock was intended to allow boats to either enter the Chemung River or exit the river and enter the canal. The lock was rarely used since the river level was usually too low to allow the lock to be used. The spillway lock had to lower a boat over 13 feet to the river level. The water from the spillway lock ran through a sluice under Water Street and into the river. (Chemung County Historical Society)

the Chemung Canal opened, the locks had been a constant headache. The decision to use wooden rather than stone locks saved money in the short run, but over the canal's life the wooden locks proved very costly. The wooden locks lacked the strength and durability to handle the water pressure and elements. After only one year in operation, the canal commissioners had already noted problems with the locks. In their 1835 report to the legislature they stated: "On this canal of 40 miles are 51 lift locks in operation . . . . Constructed of wood, more care is necessary in locking than in the common stone lock; and the numerous short levels are liable to much derangement. Under these circumstances the expense of lock tending is inevitably great."[28]

By 1840, it had become apparent that the locks had to be replaced. People in Elmira expressed concern that the lock conditions could require forfeiting an entire shipping season to make the necessary repairs. On March 14, 1840, citizens met in Elmira to draft a resolution to the state legislature, urging that action be taken to prevent the canal's collapse. The legislature responded by appropriating $100,000 to rebuild the locks on the Chemung Canal.[29]

The canal commissioners met in Jefferson (Watkins Glen) in July 1840 to consider plans to replace the locks. The commissioners had an opportunity to rectify the lock troubles, but the decision they made would only add to them. One plan called for using composite locks made with wood and stone that would be the same size (90 feet by 15 feet) as the old locks. Estimates projected that composite locks built to that size would cost $7,263 each. A second proposal called for timber locks, using the same dimensions and costing $4,390 each. The third plan sought to have composite locks the same size as the proposed Erie enlarged locks (18 feet by 110 feet), which would cost $11,536. The final plan suggested enlarged size timber locks for $5,803 each. The commissioners realized that building composite locks using the enlarged size would be very expensive. In fact, the expense would have exceeded what it had cost to build the entire canal. The commissioners also decided that building enlarged locks would not be practical unless the Erie Canal and the Cayuga and Seneca Canal were already enlarged. In the end, they decided to remain with timber locks based on the original size.[30]

Unfortunately for the Chemung Canal, that decision proved to be short-sighted. The Erie and Cayuga and Seneca Canals were later enlarged, making them able to handle bigger boats and also more able to compete with the railroads when they arrived. The Chemung Canal found itself forced to remain with smaller boats. In fact, cargoes frequently had to be transferred from the smaller Chemung boats to the larger Erie boats before being towed north on Seneca Lake to the Cayuga and Seneca Canal at Geneva. This proved inefficient and troublesome and later encouraged shipping coal and lumber by rail to avoid transshipment from one canal boat to another.

28 *Annual Report of the Canal Commissioners*, 1835, p. 27.
29 Whitford, *History of the Canal System*, 624–26; *Annual Report of the Canal Commissioners*, 1841, p. 58.
30 Whitford, *History of the Canal System*, 624–26; *Annual Report of the Canal Commissioners*, 1841, p. 58.

The decision to remain with wooden locks also proved to be a mistake. By selecting wooden locks, the state sought to save money, but in the long run it would cost the state more to continually rebuild the locks. In less than 10 years, the locks were once again rotting and falling apart. A more sensible plan would have been to rebuild the locks a few at a time, using composite locks that would have been more durable. If that had been done, the locks would have lasted longer and required fewer expensive repairs.

During 1841 and 1842, all but two locks on the Chemung Canal were rebuilt. They worked well for one year, and then the problems began again. The locks began bowing, making it difficult to move canal boats through them. In subsequent years, more locks exhibited the same problems. Lock 49 in Elmira, where the canal met the Chemung River, had not been replaced with the others and had deteriorated so badly it had to be replaced. By 1849, the canal commissioners realized their mistake in choosing wooden locks. The commissioners reported to the legislature in 1849: "The plan upon which these locks were rebuilt was defective. Since their construction, large expenditures have been incurred each year to maintain them in good order. These difficulties, from the perishable nature of the materials of which they are constructed, must increase yearly, until it becomes necessary to replace them by those of a more durable nature."[31]

The next year, the canal commissioners recommended that the locks be rebuilt once again. The expense of digging away the embankments on many locks each year and resetting the walls had become too great. Each season it became more difficult to get boats through the locks. The locks threatened to severely injure navigation on the canal at a time when business prepared to increase rapidly. The Erie Railroad arrived in Elmira and Corning in 1849 bringing more cargo to be hauled on the canal. The coal trade continued to increase, and plans began in 1853 to build the Junction Canal, which would bring many coal barges to the Chemung Canal. The Williamsport and Elmira Railroad had begun construction, which also promised to increase canal traffic. Corning had connections to three rail lines by 1854, with three more being constructed. The demands on the Chemung Canal were peaking while its locks were falling apart. In 1854 the state had to spend $9,000 just to keep the locks functioning for that season, yet no action appeared imminent to replace the locks.[32]

From 1850 to 1856, the canal commissioners recommended to the legislature each year that the locks on the Chemung Canal should be rebuilt using composite locks rather than wooden locks. The composite locks built with stone, cement, and wood offered greater strength. The commissioners also urged that the lock size be enlarged to match the locks on the Erie Canal and the Cayuga and Seneca Canal. The increased traffic on the Chemung Canal had proved the need for enlarged locks. The coal, lumber, and other goods that reached the Cayuga

31 *Annual Report of the Canal Commissioners*, 1844, p. 69; Ibid., 1845, p. 67; Ibid., 1846, p. 65; Ibid., 1849, p. 69.
32 Whitford, *History of the Canal System*, 629–30; *Annual Report of the Canal Commissioners*, 1850, pp. 85–86; Ibid., 1854, pp. 84–85; Ibid., 1855, p. 70.

Tolls Collected on the Chemung Canal
1833 - 1878

Year	Amount		Year	Amount
1833	$ 694.00		1857	$ 15,516.51
1834	3,178.05		1858	14,623.39
1835	4,714.98		1859	16,918.95
1836	5,066.20		1860	17,968.35
1837	4,331.60		1861	15,506.77
1838	4,394.67		1862	20,235.22
1839	5,187.27		1863	24,444.98
1840	4,958.41		1864	23,848.81
1841	9,396.42		1865	13,228.55
1842	7,702.05		1866	18,191.70
1843	9,726.56		1867	13,495.28
1844	14,385.13		1868	10,557.01
1845	21,444.53		1869	8,806.17
1846	13,503.44		1870	4,872.11
1847	16,677.32		1871	4,731.66
1848	16,191.25		1872	4,269.75
1849	15,781.34		1873	3,253.09
1850	15,997.74		1874	3,316.39
1851	15,536.92		1875	1,304.54
1852	15,848.44		1876	3,380.33
1853	19,603.18		1877	2,971.87
1854	21,152.32		1878	1,919.56
1855	19,768.42			
1856	17,117.52		**Total**	**$ 525,919.14**

Tolls collected on the Chemung Canal were dutifully reported by the toll collectors. The canal was never very profitable. Expenses nearly always exceeded the revenue collected. Over its lifetime the canal collected just over $500,000 in tolls, but required nearly $3.5 million in state expenditures to build, improve, and repair it. (Whitford, *History of the New York State Canals*)

and Seneca Canal from the Chemung Canal and Seneca Lake could easily connect to the Erie Canal without having to be loaded into bigger boats. The Junction Canal, which would connect the Chemung Canal to the North Branch Canal in Pennsylvania, included plans to use locks equivalent to the Erie locks. It only made sense that the Chemung Canal could better serve the public with enlarged locks, but not everyone agreed the Chemung Canal needed enlargement.

Some legislators balked at spending a large sum to enlarge the Chemung Canal locks. They argued that the Chemung Canal did not carry enough traffic. The enlarged locks would permit nearly three times as much tonnage per year to pass through the canal than had ever passed through it in years past. Without a sufficient amount of tonnage to produce enough revenue to repay the state for the work, why should the canal be enlarged? Second, the water supply for the existing canal had been inadequate, and enlargement would require an even greater need for water. It did not appear that the Chemung River could meet the needs required by bigger locks. The Chemung Railroad served as the third reason for opposing the Chemung Canal enlargement. It seemed unreasonable to expend money on the canal when the railroad ran right alongside it and could meet the shipping needs for the area.

The legislature voted down the bill to enlarge the Chemung Canal locks in 1856. Although the locks would not be enlarged, they still needed rebuilding as many were falling apart. In the winter of 1856–57, the canal commissioners received authorization from the legislature to rebuild the locks as needed. The commissioners decided to build two composite locks that winter. The cost topped $31,000. With 53 locks on the canal, replacing them all with composite locks would be too costly. The commissioners once again turned to wooden locks.

From 1857 to 1867, the remaining locks were all gradually replaced with wooden structures. The gradual replacement meant that every season many decrepit locks still had to have the embankment stripped away to fix the walls and to have other repairs done to them. Using wood to rebuild the locks meant an imminent return to the old problems. By 1861, many newly rebuilt wooden locks became unusable when their sides bowed. Boatmen and lockkeepers had to hack

Tonnage Shipped on the Chemung Canal
1833 - 1878

Year	Tonnage	Year	Tonnage
1833	3,305	1857	187,201
1834	16,085	1858	205,168
1835	22,452	1859	256,323
1836	24,125	1860	226,323
1837	20,288	1861	208,742
1838	30,256	1862	243,628
1839	36,089	1863	307,151
1840	34,217	1864	280,834
1841	63,042	1865	164,796
1842	54,866	1866	226,510
1843	66,247	1867	145,627
1844	88,231	1868	165,875
1845	114,740	1869	245,761
1846	124,768	1870	206,535
1847	189,165	1871	173,281
1848	150,691	1872	217,263
1849	135,867	1873	257,962
1850	128,263	1874	205,602
1851	159,563	1875	129,425
1852	187,577	1876	214,448
1853	249,980	1877	12,026
1854	270,978	1878	8,767
1855	223,271		
1856	245,621	Total-	6,928,663

Toll collectors also had to report the tonnage passing through the Chemung Canal. During the Civil War years the canal witnessed record use. The demand for goods during the war led boatmen to stack up goods on the decks of the canal boats. This often led to damaged bridges along the canal route due to over-stacked boats. (Whitford, *History of the New York State Canals*)

away at some of the beams to make enough clearance to get boats in and out from the locks, which only further weakened the structures.[33]

The Chemung Canal found itself caught between a rock and a hard place. It enjoyed prosperity in the 1850s yet could not modernize to meet the rising demand. The Chemung Canal's inability to handle larger boats led businesses such as John Magee's coal business to turn to the railroads as a carrier. Had the locks been enlarged using composite locks, the Chemung Canal could have enjoyed a longer life and would have been more competitive with the railroads. Its many locks made it difficult to solve the problem. Replacing so many defective locks all at once with composite locks would be too costly. The lost effort to enlarge the Chemung Canal locks began the canal's slide into oblivion. Yet war clouds loomed in 1861, and the canal would get one more chance to serve.

With the Civil War, the demands upon the Chemung Canal became greater than they had ever been. The toll revenue collected and the tonnage shipped increased tremendously from 1862 to 1864. In 1863 tonnage passing through the canal reached its peak at 307,151 tons. The canal achieved its two highest annual toll revenue amounts in 1863 and 1864 when it collected $24,444.98 and $23,848.81, respectively. The war effort required supplies, and the nation used every possible means to ship them.

The canal enjoyed prosperity thanks to the war, but the increased demands also made its deficiencies even more apparent. The canal commissioners' report for the Chemung Canal in 1863 noted the heavy traffic on the canal and the canal's poor condition. The report said: "Most of the locks being constructed of wood many years ago have become much dilapidated, and to keep up good navigation through them at all times has been a task of considerable difficulty."[34]

Wartime needs led to the rebuilding of more locks over the next two years. Still, the canal's smaller size in relation to other canals continued to be a problem. Attempts to get more supplies through quickly to meet war demands caused boats to be overloaded. Bridges across the canal suffered damages from cargo stacked up too high on canal boats. The problem became so acute that the Canal Board passed a law to address it. The new law stipulated that boats and their cargoes could not exceed nine feet in height above the waterline.[35]

The heavily laden boats also found it difficult to get enough draft in the four-foot-deep canal, especially during the dry season. To address the need for more depth, the Canal Board authorized increasing the canal depth to six feet in 1863 to provide the boats with a four-foot draft. To achieve the new depth the canal banks were raised to allow the prism to hold more water. While this gave the boats more clearance, it did not address how to achieve the greater water volume

---

33 Whitford, *History of the Canal System*, pp. 630–31; *Annual Report of the Canal Commissioners*, 1856, pp. 66–67; Ibid., 1857, p. 82; Ibid., 1858, p. 69; Ibid., 1861, p. 80.
34 *Annual Report of the Canal Commissioners*, 1863, pp. 91–92.
35 *Havana Journal*, December 19, 1863, p. 3.

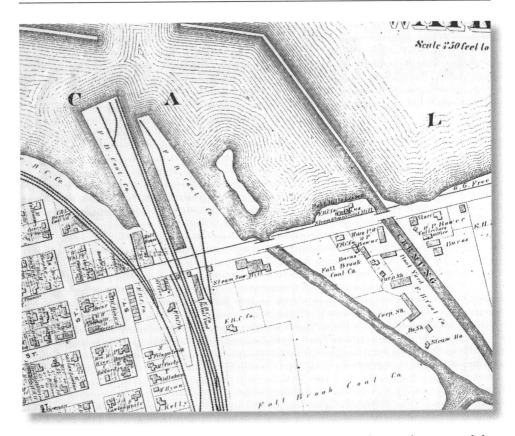

At Watkins Glen, canal boats tied up at a harbor in Seneca Lake and awaited a tow north by steamboats. At Geneva the boats locked into the Cayuga and Seneca Canal and then could enter the Erie Canal. Coal companies established works along the lake to load coal from railroad cars into canal boats. It was a common site to see a steamboat heading north on the lake with many canal boats towed behind. (*Atlas of Schuyler County, New York*. Philadelphia: Pomeroy, Whitman and Company, 1874. Montour Falls Memorial Library)

the canal would require. Discussions about using Mud Lake and Little Lake as reservoirs resumed but still did not lead to any action.[36]

The war's demand for coal accentuated another weakness of the Chemung Canal. The canal's inability to handle larger boats had already resulted in more coal being hauled on the Chemung Railroad, which ran beside the Chemung Canal to Jefferson. The canal commissioners pointed out in 1864 that if the Chemung Canal were enlarged, it could realize greater toll revenue from carrying virtually all the coal trade. Failure to enlarge could prove fatal to the canal. As the commissioners noted, "If this work [enlargement] cannot be undertaken immediately, it is certain that one or more new lines of railroad must and will be constructed to accommodate this important trade."[37]

The increased business the war brought to the canal also presented problems at the canal's terminus at Seneca Lake. Canal boats gathered along the lake

36 Whitford, *History of the Canal System*, 634; *Annual Report of the Canal Commissioners*, 1864, p. 68.
37 *Annual Report of the Canal Commissioners*, 1864, p. 69.

shore to be towed north to Geneva by steamboats. Construction of a pier to help protect the boats had begun in 1859 but had never been finished due to a dispute with the contractor. The state saw to it that the pier was completed in 1861. Trestle works allowed railway cars loaded with coal to have their contents emptied into canal barges. The enlarged Cayuga and Seneca Canal at the north end of the lake in Geneva drew off more water and lowered Seneca Lake. The lower lake level and the sandbars caused by waves made the lake too shallow at the harbor where the canal boats tied up. This made it difficult for the steamboats to get close enough to the boats to affix the towline. Two thousand dollars had to be spent to dredge the lake in 1863.[38]

The repairs made during the Civil War and the ever-rising demand for coal kept the Chemung Canal functioning in the years after the war. During the war, many locks had been rebuilt, and the canal depth increased to allow for heavier loads. The coal trade precipitated the improvements at Watkins Glen to improve the piers and breakwater. In 1869, in one of the briefest reports about the canal on record, the canal commissioners' report for the Chemung Canal said: "This canal is unquestionably in better condition than ever before. Its locks have all been rebuilt, and its prism and banks put in proper condition. The structures are in good repair and navigation during the season has been complete."[39]

Even though the canal seemed in good shape and tonnages from 1865 to 1874 often topped the 200,000 mark, all was not well with the Chemung Canal. Toll revenue continued to decrease. The Civil War had done a great deal to promote the railroads. Rail lines proliferated and began to surpass canal shipping. Coal mine owners bought and built railroads to ship their coal. John Magee had his own railroad bring his coal from the Fall Brook Mines to Watkins Glen, and the Morris Run Mines used rail lines to ship theirs as well. In 1868 tolls collected on the Chemung Canal only amounted to $10,500, and after 1869 they never exceeded $5,000 in any year. The tolls collected in the canal's final decade amounted to less than the tolls collected in the years 1862 and 1863.[40]

The greater availability of railroads began to impact the canal. The census for the town of Montour in Schuyler County in 1865 and 1875, which included Havana, reflected the canal's decline in that town. In 1865, 15 men listed their occupation as boatman. Ten years later only one person claimed that occupation.[41]

One by one, the smaller canals began to fold when confronted by greater railroad competition. The Junction Canal, which had brought coal from Pennsylvania to the Chemung Canal, closed in 1871. The Junction Canal's lifeline to the coal fields, the North Branch Canal, had been so heavily damaged by a flood

38 Whitford, *History of the Canal System*, pp. 634–35; *Annual Report of the Canal Commissioners*, 1862, pp. 80–81; Ibid., 1864, p. 70.
39 *Annual Report of the Canal Commissioners*, 1869, p. 48.
40 Whitford, *History of the Canal System*, pp. 1064–65.
41 *Town of Montour Census*, 1865, 1875, Schuyler County Historical Society.

in 1865 that Pennsylvania chose not to rebuild it. Soon a railroad ran on the bank along the abandoned North Branch Canal. Since coal had been the main commodity shipped on the Junction Canal, the North Branch Canal closing spelled the end for the Junction Canal as well. A company known as the Junction Canal and Railroad Company bought the Junction Canal and built a railroad along its route.[42] Railroads were winning the battle to control shipping.

The annual cost to repair the lateral canals, including the Chemung Canal, far exceeded the revenues they returned. In a report about the lateral canals made in 1872, Canal Commissioner William Wright made clear that the lateral canals had outlived their usefulness and become a liability. Wright explained that the railroads, which in many cases ran alongside the canals, could more efficiently transport goods. He also pointed out that the wooden locks had deteriorated so badly that almost all needed replacing once again. The considerable cost to replace them, when added to annual maintenance expenses, would only serve to drain away taxpayer money. What about the added business the lateral canals brought to the Erie? Wright pointed out that after the Erie enlargement the smaller lateral canals could no longer contribute much business to the Erie because the lateral canals could not handle the larger boats. Erie Canal enlargements had allowed it to remain in competition with the railroads. Without similar enlargements on the lateral canals, those canals had little hope of competing with the railways.

Wright concluded his report by raising the prospect that with little hope existing to revive the lateral canals, future expenditures on the lateral canals should be suspended until a new policy could be formulated about what should be done with them.[43] The commissioners did not follow Wright's advice. They did not suspend expenditures on the lateral canals, and the costs continued to mount. In 1872, the same year that Mr. Wright gave his assessment, the state spent over $112,000 to repair and operate the Chemung Canal. That same year the Chemung Canal collected less than $4,300 in tolls. Even though the cost to maintain the Chemung Canal decreased in the years after that due to less flooding, the expenses still far exceeded the revenue.[44]

By 1876, improper maintenance had left the Chemung Canal in poor condition. The locks and aqueducts on the canal became very run-down. Eel grass that had not been mowed from the prism had grown so thick that navigation had to be suspended for two weeks until it could be cut. The canal's condition made it unlikely that it would be navigable much longer without substantial repairs, which were not forthcoming. With the Syracuse, Geneva, and Corning Railroad anticipated to be completed soon, the commissioners' report regarded the Chemung

42 Whitford, *History of the Canal System*, pp. 1063–65, p. 758.
43 William Wright, "The Lateral Canals on the Middle Division," *Annual Report of the Canal Commissioners*, 1872, pp. 95–97.
44 Whitford, *History of the Canal System*, p. 1065; *Annual Report of the Canal Commissioners*, 1873, p. 87; Ibid., 1874, p. 104.

Canal "as one of the unfortunate 'limbs of the commercial tree,' which it would be best for the legislative 'ax-man' to lop off."[45]

The ax-man's blade did fall. The canal commissioners' report in 1877 announced that the Chemung Canal no longer warranted the expenditure of public monies. The legislature passed a law in 1877 closing the canal after the 1878 season. The canal handled very little business its last two seasons, with a few lumber shipments providing the most revenues. A report on the lateral canals in 1877 said about the Chemung Canal: "the railroads contiguous to it have attracted to themselves nearly or quite all the business of the country, and by affording greater facilities to forwarders have rendered the canal, for general purposes, and particularly for coal, worthless and unused."[46] The canal closed on October 31, 1878. The Chemung Canal era had ended.

But for a series of missed opportunities, the life of the Chemung Canal might have been prolonged. When faced with the need to replace the crumbling locks, the state had decided to save money and build more wooden locks. By the 1870s, rather than bear the expense of rebuilding many of the locks for the third time, the state chose to save money by abandoning the Chemung Canal. Although locks made of stone were expensive, they would have proved more durable and perhaps cheaper than wooden locks in the long run.

The final chapter for the Chemung Canal came in 1880 when the stone and other materials used in the locks, bridges, and aqueducts were sold off at an auction held at Corning. An amendment to the state constitution in 1846 had stipulated that the canals were to remain state property forever; however, an amendment in 1874 removed the restriction, as the state anticipated the need to dispose with the lateral canals. The amendment paved the way to the auction block for the Chemung Canal. The sale yielded $2,200 from the stone and iron in the canal works.

The towns and villages through which the canal passed received the rights to the canal prism within their limits. Other parts were sold to private citizens along the canal route or to railroads. The Canal Railroad Company based in Elmira bought a section that ran from Elmira to where the canal intersected the Utica, Ithaca, and Elmira Railroad in Horseheads.[47]

The canal became a nuisance to the communities it once served. The bridges that carried traffic over the canal had always been a problem. Like the canal, they had required constant expense to keep them in good condition. Some were swing bridges, which often caused injuries to citizens. When they were not properly swung back into place, people fell many feet into the canal below when they tried to cross them at night. In 1865 the daughter of the army surgeon at

---

45 *Annual Report of the Canal Commissioners*, 1876, pp. 98–99; Ibid., 1877, p. 116.
46 *Annual Report of the Canal Commissioners*, 1877, p. 116; Whitford, *History of the Canal System*, p. 637; "The Chemung Canal," *The Havana Journal*, January 27, 1877, p. 3; October 12, 1887, p. 3.
47 Whitford, *History of the Canal System*, pp. 637–38.

the Elmira Prison Camp suffered serious injuries when she fell through a swing bridge in Elmira that had not been properly closed. A woman in Havana suffered two fractured ribs when she shared the same fate at an unfinished swing bridge over the canal at South Street in 1853.[48]

When the canal went into decline, the bridges numbered among the first fixtures to be removed. In 1871 Elmira sought permission from the state legislature to remove the bridges and fill in the canal for nearly a mile to form a city street. Most businesses along that section had moved on, and it made sense to save money by dismantling the bridges rather than pay for their upkeep. In 1872 the legislature passed the necessary law to allow Elmira to create a street by filling in the canal prism from the point where it met the Junction Canal to the Chemung River.[49]

A larger and more deadly problem came from the fetid water languishing in the canal bed. An unfortunate family in Elmira lost three children in one week to diphtheria in September 1878. Health investigators attributed the source to the stagnant water in the Chemung Canal near their home. The water had become filled with filth and dead animals. The sewage from the Elmira Reformatory emptied directly into the canal. Buildups in the canal bed acted as dams that kept the water from flowing, allowing the filth to accumulate. Forty people died from diseases in Elmira in July and 48 more in August, many from diphtheria and cholera. The citizens in Elmira demanded action. The city cleaned out the canal prism and mowed the grass growing in it. With the water flow restored, the problem abated; however, the city permitted the Reformatory sewer to continue emptying into the canal.[50]

Havana faced a similar problem with the canal bed that ran through its village. The canal became choked with vegetation and foul water. One Havana resident referred to the abandoned canal as a "stagnant miasmatic pond." In 1881 the village took steps to fill in the canal bed through the village up to lock one. The canal from lock one to Seneca Lake remained open as some businessmen hoped to continue using that portion. Today it harbors a marina, and boats can still travel its waters to reach Seneca Lake. In 1885 the state legislature appropriated $10,000 to drain the canal prism from Horseheads to Havana.[51]

Just as the canal's arrival had transformed the towns along its banks, its disappearance had an important impact. The Chemung Canal had stimulated the economies and increased the populations in the towns it served. With the canal's abandonment business slumped, and people moved on. Only a few months after the canal's final closing, a Havana resident wrote in an editorial: "What shall be

---

48 *Elmira Sunday Telegram*, January 30, 1921, reprint in "The Chemung Canal," *Chemung Historical Journal*, vol. 1, no. 4 (June, 1956): p. 152; *Havana Journal*, September 10, 1853, p. 2.
49 Whitford, *History of the Canal System*, p. 636.
50 *Elmira Daily Advertiser*, September 16, 1878, p. 5; September 17, 1878, p. 4; September 18, 1878, p. 4; September 19, 1878, p. 4; September 24, 1878, p. 4.
51 Morrison, ed., *Early History, &c., Havana, New York*, 234; *Havana Journal*, January 25, 1879, p. 3; May 14, 1881, p. 3.

done for the prosperity of Havana, is a question which appears to be deeply engaging the attention of her most thoughtful citizens. Can anything be done to revive the commercial interests of the village, and set in motion the wheels of thrift, enterprise and industry, and give steady employment to our mechanics and laboring people . . . ?"[52] The boatyards were folding, the pottery works had gone out of business, and the village's population had declined by 100 people since 1860. The railroad passed through Havana, but the village never became an important stop on the line. Havana had been a canal town, but it never became a railroad town. The town suffered due to the canal's closing.

Watkins Glen also witnessed a decline once the canal era ended. The railroad once brought cars filled with coal to be transshipped into canal boats on Seneca Lake. Now the railcars merely passed through Watkins Glen, heading north on the Syracuse, Geneva and Corning Railroad. Even before the canal closed, the slowing business led the *Watkins Express* to comment in 1869 that Watkins Glen would not grow if it could not attract some industry. The coal industry did not provide enough jobs to local people, and without some manufacturing interests the village could not hope to attract more people.

The Schuyler County population peaked in 1880 with 18,842 residents. It then began a decline that lasted until the 1950s. By 1890 there were 2,000 fewer residents. In 1910 only 14,000 people remained in the county. The tax rolls also reflected the county's decline. In 1867 Schuyler County collected $142,000 in taxes. In 1876 it collected half that amount.[53]

Not all the former Chemung Canal towns had been hurt by the closing. Elmira and Corning became important stops on railroad lines and developed manufacturing interests. In 1868 the Brooklyn Flint Glass Works relocated to Corning. By the following year it employed nearly 150 men. This began what is today Corning Incorporated. In 1871 Simon Ingersoll experimented with rock drills. His efforts led to the Ingersoll-Rand Company in Painted Post. The Fall Brook Railroad had repair shops in Corning. The Corning Brick Works opened in 1878. Other manufacturing interests opened in Corning after the Civil War such as a farm machinery company, a stove works, foundries, and steam-powered grist mills. Corning became an industrial town after the Civil War.[54]

Elmira also developed more industry. The Rolling Mills continued to manufacture iron until the 1890s. In 1873 the LaFrance Fire Engine Company began operations in Elmira. It later became the American-LaFrance Company and at one time ranked among the largest fire engine manufacturers in the United States. The Elmira Bridge Company opened on the south side in 1889, and the

52 *Havana Journal*, March 8, 1879, p. 3.
53 *Watkins Express*, March 4, 1869, p.2; *Schuyler County: The First Hundred Years, 1854–1954*, p. 58, pp. 60–61, Schuyler County Historical Society; *History of Schuyler County, New York* (Philadelphia: J. B. Lipincott and Company, 1879), p. 51.
54 Dimitroff and Janes, *History of the Corning-Painted Post Area*, pp. 60–61, pp. 75–78.

F. M. Howell Company began manufacturing wooden boxes for cigars and other products in 1883.[55]

The Chemung Canal, once the centerpiece for the area's economy, faded into the past as the railroads took its place. Its rather short life could lead one to conclude that it had been a failure. The annual losses due to the high repair and maintenance expenses contribute to that argument. Yet the canal provided a vital service at an important time. With the railroads still nearly 20 years in the future, the Chemung Canal opened a market economy that brought prosperity and economic growth. Although the canal had not been a financial success, the area owed a great deal to its existence. The canal changed the landscape, the economy, and the population in the region. A canal culture arose that centered around the canal's seasonal operation. When a better transportation method became available, it was inevitable that the canal would have to yield its place. The canal culture gave way to a railroad culture. The railroad brought speed and year-round operation, but it also enhanced much that the canal had introduced: jobs, a better means to move goods, more immigrant residents, and more industry.

Would the canal have fared better as a private enterprise much like the railroads? Probably not. The short distance the canal spanned and the high costs involved to maintain it would likely have meant an even shorter life as a private business. Even with the vast resources available as part of a large public canal system, the Chemung Canal could not be profitable. The Junction Canal found it could not survive as a private enterprise. High costs and the railroads swallowed it up as well.

Today it is difficult to envision canal boats plying their way through Elmira, Big Flats, Horseheads, Millport, Montour Falls, and Watkins Glen, but for over 40 years they did just that. It is almost as difficult to picture Corning as a leading port in New York State.

While the railroads may have made the canal disappear, it did not vanish entirely. Many vestiges of the Chemung Canal can still be seen. Between Horseheads and Montour Falls one can still see remains of the canal prism. Sections from the feeder canal are still visible between Big Flats and Horseheads as well. While driving through Elmira, Horseheads, Big Flats, and Montour Falls one will still find a Canal Street and see offices for the Chemung Canal Bank. In Montour Falls, Charles Cook's Montour House still stands. So do the other buildings he erected in hopes of locating the Schuyler County seat in his town. From Montour Falls to Watkins Glen, boats still travel the channel that once served as the final leg on the Chemung Canal. Alongside that channel sits another silent reminder from a bygone age: an abandoned railroad bed.

55 Thomas Byrne, *Chemung County, 1890–1975* (Elmira, New York: Chemung County Historical Society, Inc., 1975), p. 285, 291, 314.

Bibliographic Essay

ALTHOUGH I FIRST THOUGHT THERE MAY be few sources of information about the Chemung Canal, I was glad to discover that there was actually a great deal of information about the canal. The New York State Archives and New York State Library in Albany provided maps and many other documents about the operation of the canal. The canal commissioners had to give a report to the legislature every year about the conditions of the state canals. All of those reports are available at the state archives. The state archives also has canal boat registrations, lockkeeper reports, and contracts for canal repairs. The New York State Archives provides a useful book identifying its holdings about canals in New York State. It is called *The Mighty Chain: A Guide to Canal Records in the New York State Archives*.

Another great source of primary documents about the Chemung Canal is contemporary newspapers. Cornell University has microfilm records of many newspapers from all across New York State. They are housed in Olin Library. The Montour Falls Memorial Library has an excellent microfilm collection of the *Havana Journal* containing a tremendous amount of information about the Chemung Canal for anyone who has the patience to scan through them. The library at Hobart College in Geneva has an indexed microfilm collection of the early 19th-century Geneva newspapers. Genevans' interest in the Chemung Canal was reflected in the many articles about the creation and progress of the canal. The Steele Memorial Library in Elmira has issues of the Elmira newspapers on microfilm. Much can be gleaned about the canal from extant Elmira newspapers, although some years are missing.

The William Bouck papers at Cornell University proved to be another valuable resource. Bouck was a canal commissioner when the Chemung Canal was built. He later was elected governor of New York State. His papers contain letters to and from the engineers in charge of constructing the Chemung Canal. The letters from engineers Holmes Hutchinson and Joseph Dana Allen reveal the many difficulties encountered while building the canal. The Bouck papers also contain letters about the construction of the Crooked Lake Canal, which was built contemporaneously with the Chemung Canal.

A useful secondary source is Noble Whitford's *History of the Canal System of New York, Together with Brief Histories of the Canals of the United States and Canada,* published in 1906. While it is mostly about the Erie Canal, Whitford included some brief histories of the various lateral canals, including the Chemung Canal. The book also contains excellent statistical information about the canals such as the annual tonnage carried and the annual toll revenue collected. A copy of the book is very difficult to find. The Steele Memorial Library in Elmira has a copy that is kept in a locked bookcase, and it is available upon request. The text of Whitford's book is also available online through a web site maintained by the University of Rochester. The web site address is **www.history.rochester.edu/canal/ bib/whitford/old1906**, or it can be reached through a link on my web site about the Chemung Canal at: **www.chemungcanal.netfirms.com.**

Two other good sources of secondary information are the Chemung County Historical Society on Water Street in Elmira and the Schuyler County Historical Society on Catharine Street in Montour Falls. Both keep many articles about the canal on file. Ausburn Towner's book, *The History of the Valley and the County of Chemung,* published in 1892, can be found at the Chemung County Historical Society, as well as at the Steele Memorial Library. Towner lived during the days of the Chemung Canal and offered valuable insights about the canal and early Elmira.

Bibliography

PRIMARY SOURCES:

Albany Argus, 1828–1830. Olin Library, Cornell University, Ithaca, New York.

Annual Report of the Canal Commissioners, 1830–1878. New York State Archives, Albany, New York.

A. Overfield to John Arnot. October 22, 1868. Arnot Family Papers. Chemung County Historical Society, Elmira, New York.

Assembly Documents, Chapter 236, April 20, 1825. New York State Library, Albany, New York.

Assembly Journal, 1835, 1837, 1847, 1853. New York State Library.

Baker, G. Newton. "Reminiscences of Captain Newton G. Baker." Folder 060–040, Pennsylvania Canals, April 22, 1951. Chemung County Historical Society, Elmira, New York.

Chemung Canal Contracts, Packet 1. New York State Archives.

The Chemung County Historical Society. Folder MC–74 John Arnot Papers.

Corning Journal, 1849–1859. Olin Library, Cornell University, Ithaca, New York.

Elmira Daily Advertiser, 1864, 1878. Steele Memorial Library, Elmira, New York.

Elmira Directory, 1863–1864. Chemung County Historical Society.

Elmira Gazette, 1830–1839, 1918. Steele Memorial Library.

Elmira Weekly Gazette, 1835. Chemung County Historical Society.

Elmira Republican, 1850. Steele Memorial Library.

Elmira Sunday Telegram, 1870, 1885, 1888, 1921, 1923, 1948, 1953. Steele Memorial Library.

Elmira Weekly Advertiser, 1859, 1864, 1867. Steele Memorial Library.

Farmers' Advocate, 1831. Steuben County Historical Society, Bath, New York.

Geneva Gazette, 1825, 1829. Hobart College, Geneva, New York.

Geneva Gazette and General Advertiser, 1826–1831. Hobart College.

Geneva Gazette and Mercantile Advertiser, 1829, 1830, 1833. Hobart College.

Geneva Palladium, 1825, 1826, 1828. Hobart College.

Havana Journal, 1849–1881. Montour Falls Memorial Library, Montour Falls, New York.

Havana Republican, 1839–1847. Montour Falls Memorial Library.

Ithaca Journal, 1829–1833. Cornell University.

Letter to the Board of Canal Commissioners from Businessmen of Havana and Elmira. March 1834. New York State Archives.

New York. Assembly. Legislative Document no. 195, February 23, 1830. New York State Library.

New York. Senate. *Senate Journal*. New York State Library, 1848.

P. J. Velie to the Canal Department of the State of New York. March 13, 1854. Series A1440, Box 2, 922. New York State Archives.

Petitions filed for damages caused by the Chemung Canal. Series A1140, Packets 26 and 27. 1833. New York State Archives.

Town of Montour Census, 1865, 1875. Schuyler County Historical Society, Montour Falls, New York.

Town of Veteran Census, 1855. Steele Memorial Library.

Watkins Express, 1869, 1952. Montour Falls Memorial Library.

William Bouck Papers, Kroch Library, Cornell University.

WORKS CITED:

Aldrich, Lewis, ed. *History of Yates County, New York*. Syracuse, New York: D. Mason and Company, 1892.

Bell, Barbara, ed. *Diary of Gilbert Hillerman*. Schuyler County Historical Society, Montour Falls, New York.

Biographical Directory of the United States Congress, 1774–Present. http://bioguide. congress.gov. Accessed March 2000.

Byrne, Thomas. *Chemung County, 1890–1975*. Elmira, New York: Chemung County Historical Society, Inc., 1975.

Chandler, Alfred D. Jr. *The Railroads: The Nation's First Big Business*. New York: Harcourt, Brace, and World, Inc., 1965.

"The Chemung Canal." *The Chemung Historical Journal,* vol. 1, no. 4 (June 1956): 143–176.

Chemung County . . . Its History, ed. Writers' Group of the Chemung County Historical Society. Elmira, New York: Chemung County Historical Society, 1961.

The Chemung County Historical Society. Folders 060–020 Chemung Canal; CF– 0640 Chemung Canal; CWP–28 Chemung Canal; 325–400 Towns of Chemung, Millport; VF135–025 and C–1410 Irish.

Clayton, W. W. *History of Steuben County, New York*. Philadelphia: Lewis, Peck, and Co., 1879.

Dimitroff, Thomas and Lois Janes. *History of the Corning-Painted Post Area*, Corning, New York: Corning Area Bicentennial Committee, 1977.

Fitzpatrick, John, ed. *The Diaries of George Washington*. Vol. 2. New York: Houghton Mifflin Company, 1935.

French, J. H. *Gazetteer of the State of New York*. Port Washington, New York: Ira Friedman, Inc., 1860.

Galpin, W. Freeman. *Central New York: An Inland Empire*. New York: Lewis Historical Publishing Company, Inc., 1941.

Garey, Carl B. *Legacies From Queen Catharine Montour and Charles Cook: A History of Montour and Montour Falls, New York*. 1974. Montour Falls Memorial Library, Montour Falls, New York.

Goodrich, Carter, ed. *Canals and American Economic Development*. Port Washington, New York: Kennikat Press, 1972.

Goodrich, Carter. *Government Promotion of American Canals and Railroads*. New York: Columbia University Press, 1960.

Gordon, Thomas. *Gazetteer of the State of New York*. Philadelphia: Collins Printers,
1836.

Gusfield, Joseph. *Symbolic Crusade: Status Politics and the American Temperance Movement*. Chicago: University of Illinois Press, 1986.

Hepburn, A. Barton. *Artificial Waterways and Commercial Development*. New York: MacMillan Company, 1909.

The Historical Letters of Uncle Jonas Lawrence. Elmira, New York: Elmira Advertisers Association, 1886.

History of Schuyler County, New York. Philadelphia: J. B. Lipincott and Company, 1879.

History of Tioga County, Pennsylvania. New York: W. W. Munsel and Company, 1883.

Holt, Michael. *The Rise and Fall of the American Whig Party*. New York: Oxford University Press, 1999.

Johnson, Paul. *A Shopkeeper's Millennium: Society and Revivals in Rochester, New York, 1815–1837*. New York: Hill and Wang, 1978.

Kingman, Leroy, ed. *Our County and its People: A Memorial History of Tioga County, New York*. Elmira, New York: W. A. Fergusson and Company, 1896.

Larkin, Daniel. *New York State Canals: A Short History*. Fleischmanns, New York: Purple Mountain Press, 1998.

Lincoln, Charles Z., ed. *Messages From the Governors, State of New York*. Vol. II. Albany: J. B. Lyon Company, 1909.

Linehan, Mary Clare. "A History of the Irish in the City of Elmira, New York" *Elmira College Bulletin* (August, 1925). Chemung County Historical Society.

Martin, Albro. *Railroads Triumphant*. New York: Oxford University Press, 1992.

McGregor, Robert. "Radical Environmental Change: Deforestation in the Upper Delaware River Valley, 1800–1875." PhD. diss., Binghamton University, 1984.

McTiernan, Ellen. "Our Melting Pot: Eight Minorities." Folder 135–025, Ethnic Groups. Chemung County Historical Society.

Miller, Nathan. *The Enterprise of a Free People: Aspects of Economic Development in New York State during the Canal Period, 1792–1838*. Ithaca, New York: Cornell University Press, 1962.

Morrison, Wayne, ed. *Early History, &c., Havana, New York*. Ovid, New York: Morrison and Son Printers, no date.

Patton, Spiro. "Canals in American Business and Economic History: A Review of the Issues." *Canal History and Technology Proceedings* (March 28, 1987): 3–25.

Perillo, Charles. "The Junction Canal (1855–1871)." *Canal History and Technology Proceedings*, Vol. X (1991): 181–211.

Pierce, H. B., and D. Hamilton Hurd. *History of Tioga, Chemung, Tompkins, and Schuyler Counties*. Philadelphia: J. B. Lippincott and Company, 1879.

Roediger, David. *The Wages of Whiteness: Race and the Making of the American Working Class*. New York: Verso Publishing, 1991.

Rorabaugh, W. J. *The Alcoholic Republic*. New York: Oxford University Press, 1979.

Ryan, Mary. *Cradle of the Middle Class: The Family in Oneida County, New York. 1790–1865*. Cambridge: Cambridge University Press, 1981.

Schuyler County Historical Society. Folders on "Canals," "Chemung Canal," "Havana Before 1900."

Sellers, Charles. *The Market Revolution: Jacksonian America, 1815–1846*. New York: Oxford University Press, 1991.

Sheriff, Carol. *The Artificial River*. New York: Hill and Wang, 1996.

Smith, Ray. *The Political and Governmental History of the State of New York*. Syracuse, New York: Syracuse Press, 1922.

Taylor, George Rogers. *The Transportation Revolution, 1815–1860*. Vol. IV, *The Economic History of the United States*. New York: Harper and Row, 1951.

Tobin, Catherine. "Irish Labor on American Canals." *Canal History and Technology Proceedings* (March 17, 1990): 163–186.

Tomlison, Lois. "The Chemung Canal System." Craig Williams File. New York State Archives.

Towner, Ausburn. *The History of the Valley and the County of Chemung*. Syracuse, New York: D. Mason and Company, 1892.

Wager, Daniel, ed. *Our County and its People: A Descriptive Work on Oneida County, New York*. Boston: The Boston History Company, 1892.

Way, Peter. *Common Labor: Workers and the Digging of North American Canals, 1780–1860*. Baltimore: Johns Hopkins University Press, 1993.

Way, Peter. "Evil Humor and Ardent Spirits: The Rough Culture of Canal Construction Laborers." *The Journal of American History* (March 1993): 1397–1428.

Whitford, Noble. *History of the Canal System of the State of New York, Together with Brief Histories of the Canals of the United States and Canada*. Albany: Brandow Printing Company, 1906.

Whitford, Noble E. "The Cayuga and Seneca Canal." In *History of the Canal System of the State of New York*. 1906. http://www.history.rochester.edu/canal/bib/whitford/old1906/chapter8.htm. Accessed March 2000.

Williams, Craig. *Field Trip Guide, October 31, 1998, The Chemung Canal*. The Canal Society of New York State, 1998.